SELF-CONTROL

ITS KINGSHIP AND MAJESTY

BY

WILLIAM GEORGE JORDAN

British Library Cataloguing-in-Publication Data
A catalogue record for this book is available from the
British Library

CONTENTS

William George Jordan

William George Jordan was born on 6 March 1864 in New York City, USA. He took his university education at the *City College of New York* and began his literary career as an editor of *Book Chat* in 1884. After a brief spell (1888-91) editing *Current Literature* - a magazine offering an eclectic combination of literature review and contemporary commentary, Jordan relocated to Chicago. It was here that he first lectured on his system of Mental Training; although not with any great success. In 1897 Jordan moved back to New York and was hired as the managing editor for *The Ladies Home Journal*, after which he moved on to edit *The Saturday Evening Post*. This substantial editing career is not Jordan's best known achievement however – his essays and thoughts on education and 'mental training' have garnered the most attention. In July 1891 *The Chicago Inter-Ocean* printed an interview with Jordan on his 'mental training'. After the article was published he received so many inquiries that he scheduled a long lecture tour on the subject. *The Inter-Ocean* reported that 'during the past few weeks the calls from Chicago have been so numerous, enthusiastic and positive for lecture courses and private society classes that he has concluded to resign his position in New York and come to Chicago.' In 1894, Jordan published a short pamphlet; *Mental Training, A Remedy for Education,* which opened with the following lines; 'here are two great things that education should do for the individual—it should train his senses, and teach him to think. Education, as we know it to-day, does not truly do either; it gives the individual only a vast accumulation of facts, unclassified, undigested, and seen in no true relations. Like seeds kept in a box, they may be retained, but they do not grow.' Jordan's allegorical style was widely utilised in all his works, and he penned his first book, *The Kingship of Self-Control,* in 1898. This was followed by a further nine texts, all on the subject of self-improvement; a theme which he continued writing on for the rest of his life. *The Majesty of Calmness* (1900) was perhaps his most popular self-help book. Despite these successes, Jordan's most influential writing was actually a political tract. In *The House of Governors* (1907), he aimed to 'promote uniform legislation on vital questions, to conserve states' rights, to lessen centralisation, to secure a fuller, freer voice of the people and to make a stronger nation.' The work was circulated to each state governor and to President Theodore Roosevelt, and was incredibly well received. His ideas were put into practice and the first 'meeting of the governors' was held in Washington, on 18 January, 1910 – with Jordan as its secretary. He was dropped as secretary a year later, but nevertheless, this group is a key part of his legacy.

At the age of fifty-eight, Jordan married Nellie Blanche Mitchell, in New York City at the Grace Episcopal Church. The marriage was a happy one, for the short time it lasted, but sadly Jordan died just six years later of pneumonia on 20 April 1928, at his home in New York.

SELF-CONTROL

I

The Kingship *of* Self-Control

MAN has two creators,—his God and himself. His first creator furnishes him the raw material of his life and the laws in conformity with which he can make that life what he will. His second creator,—himself,—has marvellous powers he rarely realizes. It is what a man makes of himself that counts.

When a man fails in life he usually says, "I am as God made me." When he succeeds he proudly proclaims himself a "self-made man." Man is placed into this world not as a finality,—but as a possibility. Man's greatest enemy is,—himself. Man in his weakness is the creature of circumstances; man in his strength is the creator of circumstances. Whether he be victim or victor depends largely on himself.

Man is never truly great merely for what he *is*, but ever for what he may become. Until man be truly filled with the knowledge of the majesty of his possibility, until there come to him the glow of realization of his privilege to live

5

the life committed to him, as an individual life for which he is individually responsible, he is merely groping through the years.

To see his life as he might make it, man must go up alone into the mountains of spiritual thought as Christ went alone into the Garden, leaving the world to get strength to live in the world. He must there breathe the fresh, pure air of recognition of his divine importance as an individual, and with mind purified and tingling with new strength he must approach the problems of his daily living.

Man needs less of the "I am a feeble worm of the dust" idea in his theology, and more of the conception "I am a great human soul with marvellous possibilities" as a vital element in his daily working religion. With this broadening, stimulating view of life, he sees how he may attain his kingship through self-control. And the self-control that is seen in the most spectacular instances in history, and in the simplest phases of daily life, is precisely the same in kind and in quality, differing only in degree. This control man can attain, if he only will; it is but a matter of paying the price.

The power of self-control is one of the great qualities that differentiates man from the lower animals. He is the only animal capable of a moral struggle or a moral conquest.

Every step in the progress of the world has been a new "control." It has been escaping from the tyranny of a fact, to the understanding and mastery of that fact. For ages man looked in terror at the lightning flash; today he has begun to understand it as electricity, a force he has mastered and made his slave. The million phases of electrical invention are but manifestations of our control over a great force. But the greatest of all "control" is self-control.

At each moment of man's life he is either a King or a slave. As he surrenders to a wrong appetite, to any human weakness; as he falls prostrate in hopeless subjection to any condition, to any environment, to any failure, he is a slave. As he day by day crushes out human weakness, masters opposing elements within him, and day by day re-creates a new self from the sin and folly of his past,—then he is a King. He is a King ruling with wisdom over himself. Alexander conquered the whole world except,—Alexander. Emperor of the earth, he was the servile slave of his own passions.

We look with envy upon the possessions of others and wish they were our own. Sometimes we feel this in a vague, dreamy way with no thought of real attainment, as when we wish we had Queen Victoria's crown, or Emperor William's self-satisfaction. Sometimes, however, we grow bitter, storm at the wrong distribution of the good things of life, and then relapse into a hopeless fatalistic acceptance of our condition.

We envy the success of others, when we should emulate the process by which that success came. We see the splendid physical development of Sandow, yet we forget that as a babe and child he was so weak there was little hope that his life might be spared.

We may sometimes envy the power and spiritual strength of a Paul, without realizing the weak Saul of Tarsus from which he was transformed through his self-control.

We shut our eyes to the thousands of instances of the world's successes,—mental, moral, physical, financial or spiritual,—wherein the great final success came from a beginning far weaker and poorer than our own.

Any man may attain self-control if he only will. He must not expect to gain it save by long continued payment of price, in small progressive expenditures of energy. Nature is a thorough believer in the installment plan in her relations with the individual. No man is so poor that he cannot *begin* to pay for what he wants, and every small, individual payment that he makes, Nature stores and accumulates for him as a reserve fund in his hour of need.

The patience man expends in bearing the little trials of his daily life Nature stores for him as a wondrous reserve in a crisis of life. With Nature, the mental, the physical or the moral energy he expends daily in right-doing is all stored for him and transmuted into strength. Nature never accepts a cash payment in full for anything,—this would be an injustice to the poor and to the weak.

It is only the progressive installment plan Nature recognizes. No man can make a habit in a moment or break it in a moment. It is a matter of development, of growth. But at any moment man may *begin* to make or begin to break any habit. This view of the growth of character should be a mighty stimulus to the man who sincerely desires and determines to live nearer to the limit of his possibilities.

Self-control may be developed in precisely the same manner as we tone up a weak muscle,—by little exercises day by day. Let us each day do, as mere exercises of discipline in moral gymnastics, a few acts that are disagreeable to us, the doing of which will help us in instant action in our hour of need. The exercises may be very simple—dropping for a time an intensely interesting book at the most thrilling page of the story; jumping out of bed at the first moment of waking; walking home when one is perfectly able to do so, but when the temptation is to take a car; talking to some disagreeable person and trying to make the conversation pleasant. These daily exercises in moral discipline will have a wondrous tonic effect on man's whole moral nature.

The individual can attain self-control in great things only through self-control in little things. He must study himself to discover what is the weak point in his armor, what is the element within him that ever keeps him from his fullest success. This is the characteristic upon which he should begin his exercise in self-control. Is it selfishness, vanity, cowardice, morbidness, temper, laziness, worry, mind-wandering, lack of purpose?—whatever form human weakness assumes in the masquerade of life he must discover. He must then live each day as if his whole existence were telescoped down to the single day before him. With no useless regret for the past, no useless worry for the future, he should live that day as if it were his only day,—the only day left for him to assert all that is best in him, the only day left for him to conquer all that is worst in him. He should master the weak element within him at each slight manifestation from moment to moment. Each moment then must be a victory for it or for him. Will he be King, or will he be slave?—the answer rests with him.

II

The Crimes *of the* Tongue

THE second most deadly instrument of destruction is the dynamite gun,—the first is the human tongue. The gun merely kills bodies; the tongue kills reputations and, ofttimes, ruins characters. Each gun works alone; each loaded tongue has a hundred accomplices. The havoc of the gun is visible at once. The full evil of the tongue lives through all the years; even the eye of Omniscience might grow tired in tracing it to its finality.

The crimes of the tongue are words of unkindness, of anger, of malice, of envy, of bitterness, of harsh criticism, gossip, lying and scandal. Theft and murder are awful crimes, yet in any single year the aggregate sorrow, pain and suffering they cause in a nation is microscopic when compared with the sorrows that come from the crimes of the tongue. Place in one of the scale-pans of Justice the evils resulting from the acts of criminals, and in the other the grief and tears and suffering resulting from the crimes of respectability, and you will start back in amazement as you see the scale you thought the heavier shoot high in air.

At the hands of thief or murderer few of us suffer, even indirectly. But from the careless tongue of friend, the cruel tongue of enemy, who is free? No human being can live a life so true, so fair, so pure as to be beyond the reach of malice, or immune from the poisonous emanations of envy. The insidious attacks against one's reputation, the loathsome innuendoes, slurs, half-lies, by which jealous mediocrity seeks to ruin its superiors, are like those insect parasites that kill the heart and life of a mighty oak. So cowardly is the method, so stealthy the shooting of the poisoned thorns, so insignificant the separate acts in their seeming, that one is not on guard against them. It is easier to dodge an elephant than a microbe.

In London they have recently formed an Anti-Scandal League. The members promise to combat in every way in their power "the prevalent custom of talking scandal, the terrible and unending consequences of which are not generally estimated."

Scandal is one of the crimes of the tongue, but it is only one. Every individual who breathes a word of scandal is an active stockholder in a society for the spread of moral contagion. He is instantly punished by Nature by having his mental eyes dimmed to sweetness and purity, and his mind deadened to the sunlight and glow of charity. There is developed a wondrous, ingenious perversion of mental vision, by which every act of others is explained and interpreted from the lowest possible motives. They become like certain carrion flies, that pass lightly over acres of rose-gardens, to feast on a piece of putrid meat. They have developed a keen scent for the foul matter upon which they feed.

There are pillows wet by sobs; there are noble hearts broken in the silence whence comes no cry of protest; there are gentle, sensitive natures seared and warped; there are old-time friends separated and walking their lonely ways with hope dead and memory but a pang; there are cruel misunderstandings that make all life look dark,—these are but a few of the sorrows that come from the crimes of the tongue.

A man may lead a life of honesty and purity, battling bravely for all he holds dearest, so firm and sure of the rightness of his life that he never thinks for an instant of the diabolic ingenuity that makes evil and evil report where naught but good really exists. A few words lightly spoken by the tongue of slander, a significant expression of the eyes, a cruel shrug of the shoulders, with a pursing of the lips,—and then, friendly hands grow cold, the accustomed smile is displaced by a sneer, and one stands alone and aloof with a dazed feeling of wonder at the vague, intangible something that has caused it all.

For this craze for scandal, sensational newspapers of to-day are largely responsible. Each newspaper is not one tongue, but a thousand or a million tongues, telling the same foul story to as many pairs of listening ears. The vultures of sensationalism scent the carcass of immorality afar off. From the uttermost parts of the earth they collect the sin, disgrace and folly of humanity, and show them bare to the world. They do not even require *facts*, for morbid memories and fertile imaginations make even the worst of the world's happenings seem tame when compared with their monstrosities of invention. These stories, and the discussions they excite, develop in readers a cheap, shrewd power of distortion of the acts of all around them.

If a rich man give a donation to some charity, they say: "He is doing it to get his name talked about,—to help his business." If he give it anonymously, they say, "Oh, it's some millionaire who is clever enough to know that refraining from giving his name will pique curiosity; he will see that the public is informed later." If he do not give to charity, they say: "Oh, he's stingy with his money, of course, like the rest of the millionaires." To the vile tongue of gossip and slander, Virtue is ever deemed but a mask, noble ideals but a pretense, generosity a bribe.

The man who stands above his fellows must expect to be the target for the envious arrows of their inferiority. It is part of the price he must pay for his advance. One of the most detestable characters in all literature is Iago.

Envious of the promotion of Cassio above his head, he hated Othello. His was one of those low natures that become absorbed in sustaining his dignity, talking of "preserving his honor,"—forgetting it has so long been dead that even embalming could not preserve it. Day by day Iago dropped his poison; day by day did subtle resentment and studied vengeance distill the poison of distrust and suspicion into more powerfully insidious doses. With a mind wonderfully concentrated by the blackness of his purpose, he wove a network of circumstantial evidence around the pure-hearted Desdemona, and then murdered her vicariously, by the hand of Othello. Her very simplicity, confidence, innocence and artlessness made Desdemona the easier mark for the diabolic tactics of Iago.

Iago still lives in the hearts of thousands, who have all his despicable meanness without his cleverness. The constant dropping of their lying words of malice and envy have in too many instances at last worn away the noble reputations of their superiors.

To sustain ourselves in our own hasty judgments we sometimes say, as we listen, and accept without investigation, the words of these modern Iagos: "Well, where there is so much smoke, there must be *some* fire." Yes, but the fire may be only the fire of malice, the incendiary firing of the reputation of another by the lighted torch of envy, thrown into the innocent facts of a life of superiority.

III

The Red Tape *of* Duty

DUTY is the most overlauded word in the whole vocabulary of life. Duty is the cold, bare anatomy of righteousness. Duty looks at life as a debt to be paid; love sees life as a debt to be collected. Duty is ever paying assessments; love is constantly counting its premiums.

Duty is forced, like a pump; love is spontaneous, like a fountain. Duty is prescribed and formal; it is part of the red tape of life. It means running on moral rails. It is good enough as a beginning; it is poor as a finality.

The boy who "stood on the burning deck," and who committed suicide on a technical point of obedience, has been held up to the school children of this century as a model of faithfulness to duty. The boy was the victim of a blind adherence to the red tape of duty. He was placing the whole responsibility for his acts on someone outside himself. He was helplessly waiting for instruction in the hour of emergency when he should have acted for himself. His act was an empty sacrifice. It was a useless throwing away of a human life. It did no good to the father, to the boy, to the ship, or to the nation.

The captain who goes down with his sinking vessel, when he has done everything in his power to save others and when he can save his own life without dishonor, is the victim of a false sense of duty. He is cruelly forgetful of the loved ones on shore that he is sacrificing. His death means a spectacular exit from life, the cowardly fear of an investigating committee, or a brave man's loyal, yet misguided, sense of duty. A human life, with its wondrous possibilities, is too sacred an individual trust to be thus lightly thrown into eternity.

They tell us of the "sublime nobleness" of the Roman soldier at Pompeii, whose skeleton was found centuries afterward, imbedded in the once molten lava which swept down upon the doomed city. He was still standing at one of the gates, at his post of duty, still grasping a sword in his crumbling fingers. His was a morbid faithfulness to a discipline from which a great convulsion of Nature had released him. An automaton would have stood there just as long, just as boldly, just as uselessly.

The man who gives one hour of his life to loving, consecrated service to humanity is doing higher, better, truer work in the world than an army of Roman sentinels paying useless tribute to the red tape of duty. There is in this interpretation of duty no sympathy with the man who deserts his post when needed; it is but a protest against losing the essence, the realness of true duty in worshipping the mere form.

Analyze, if you will, any of the great historic instances of loyalty to duty, and whenever they ring true you will find the presence of the real element that made the act almost divine. It was duty,—plus love. It was no mere sense of duty that made Grace Darling risk her life in the awful storm of sixty years ago, when she set out in the darkness of night, on a raging sea, to rescue the survivors of the wreck of "The Forfarshire." It was the sense of duty, warmed and vivified by a love of humanity, it was heroic courage of a heart filled with divine pity and sympathy.

Duty is a hard, mechanical process for making men do things that love would make easy. It is a poor understudy to love. It is not a high enough motive with which to inspire humanity. Duty is the body to which love is the soul. Love, in the divine alchemy of life, transmutes all duties into privileges, all responsibilities into joys.

The workman who drops his tools at the stroke of twelve, as suddenly as if he had been struck by lightning, may be doing his duty,—but he is doing nothing more. No man has made a great success of his life or a fit preparation for immortality by doing merely his duty. He must do that,—and more. If he puts love into his work, the "more" will be easy.

The nurse may watch faithfully at the bedside of a sick child as a duty. But to the mother's heart the care of the little one, in the battle against death, is never a duty; the golden mantle of love thrown over every act makes the word "duty" have a jarring sound as if it were the voice of desecration.

When a child turns out badly in later years, the parent may say, "Well, I always did my duty by him." Then it is no wonder the boy turned out wrong. "Doing his duty by his son" too often implies merely food, lodging, clothes and education supplied by the father. Why, a public institution would give that! What the boy needed most was deep draughts of love; he needed to live in an atmosphere of sweet sympathy, counsel and trust. The parent should ever be an unfailing refuge, a constant resource and inspiration, not a mere larder, or hotel, or wardrobe, or school that furnishes these necessities free. The empty boast of mere parental duty is one of the dangers of modern society.

Christianity stands forth as the one religion based on love, not duty. Christianity sweeps all duties into one word,—love. Love is the one great duty enjoined by the Christian religion. What duty creeps to laboriously, love reaches in a moment on the wings of a dove. Duty is not lost, condemned or destroyed in Christianity; it is dignified, purified and exalted and all its rough ways are made smooth by love.

The supreme instance of generosity in the world's history is not the giving of millions by someone of great name; it is the giving of a mite by a widow whose name does not appear. Behind the widow's mite was no sense of duty; it was the full, free and perfect gift of a heart filled with love. In the Bible "duty" is mentioned but five times; "love," hundreds.

19

In the conquest of any weakness in our mental or moral make-up; in the attainment of any strength; in our highest and truest relation to ourselves and to the world, let us ever make "love" our watchword, not mere "duty."

If we desire to live a life of truth and honesty, to make our word as strong as our bond, let us not expect to keep ourselves along the narrow line of truth under the constant lash of the whip of duty. Let us begin to love the truth, to fill our mind and life with the strong white light of sincerity and sterling honesty. Let us love the truth so strongly that there will develop within us, without our conscious effort, an ever-present horror of a lie.

If we desire to do good in the world, let us begin to love humanity, to realize more truly the great dominant note that sounds in every mortal, despite all the discords of life, the great natural bond of unity that makes all men brothers. Then jealousy, malice, envy, unkind words and cruel misjudging will be eclipsed and lost in the sunshine of love.

The greatest triumph of the nineteenth century is not its marvellous progress in invention; its strides in education; its conquests of the dark regions of the world; the spread of a higher mental tone throughout the earth; the wondrous increase in material comfort and wealth,—the greatest triumph of the century is not any nor all of these; it is the sweet atmosphere of Peace that is covering the nations, it is the growing closer and closer of the peoples of the earth. Peace is but the breath, the perfume, the life of love. Love is the wondrous angel of life that rolls away all the stones of sorrow and suffering from the pathway of duty.

IV

The Supreme Charity *of the* World

TRUE charity is not typified by an almsbox. The benevolence of a check book does not meet all the wants of humanity. Giving food, clothing and money to the poor is only the beginning, the kindergarten class, of real charity. Charity has higher, purer forms of manifestation. Charity is but an instinctive reaching out for justice in life. Charity seeks to smooth down the rough places of living, to bridge the chasms of human sin and folly, to feed the heart-hungry, to give strength to the struggling, to be tender with human weakness, and greatest of all, it means—obeying the Divine injunction: "Judge not."

The true symbol of the greatest charity is the scales of judgment held on high, suspended from the hand of Justice. So perfectly are they poised that they are never at rest; they dare not stop for a moment to pronounce final judgment; each second adds its grain of evidence to either side of the balance. With this ideal before him, man, conscious of his own weakness and frailty, dare not arrogate to himself the Divine prerogative of pronouncing severe or final judgment on any individual. He will seek to train mind and heart to greater keenness, purity, and delicacy in watching the trembling movement of the balance in which he weighs the characters and reputations of those around him.

It is a great pity in life that all the greatest words are most degraded. We hear people say: "I do so love to study character, in the cars and on the street." They are not studying character; they are merely observing characteristics. The study of character is not a puzzle that a man may work out over night. Character is most subtle, elusive, changing and contradictory—a strange mingling of habits, hopes, tendencies, ideals, motives, weaknesses, traditions and memories—manifest in a thousand different phases.

There is but one quality necessary for the perfect understanding of character, one quality that, if man have it, he may *dare to judge*—that is, omniscience. Most people study character as a proofreader pores over a great poem: his ears are dulled to the majesty and music of the lines, his eyes are darkened to the magic imagination of the genius of the author; that proofreader is busy watching for an inverted comma, a mis-spacing, or a wrong-font letter. He has an eye trained for the imperfections, the weaknesses. Men who pride themselves on being shrewd in discovering the weak points, the vanity, dishonesty, immorality, intrigue and pettiness of others, think they understand character. They know only part of character—they know only the depths to which some men may sink; they know not the heights to which some men may rise. An optimist is a man who has succeeded in associating with humanity for some time without becoming a cynic.

We never see the target a man aims at in life; we see only the target he hits. We judge from results, and we imagine an infinity of motives that we say must have been in his mind. No man since the creation has been able to live a life so pure and noble as to exempt him from the misjudgment of those around him. It is impossible to get aught but a distorted image from a convex or a concave mirror.

If misfortune comes to someone, people are prone to say, "It is a judgment upon him." How do they know? Have they been eavesdropping at the door of Paradise? When sorrow and failure come to us, we regard them as misdirected packages that should be delivered elsewhere. We do too much watching of our neighbor's garden, too little weeding in our own.

Bottles have been picked up at sea thousands of miles from the point where they have been cast into the waters. They have been the sport of wind and weather; carried along by ocean currents, they have reached a destination undreamed of. Our flippant, careless words of judgment of the character of someone, words lightly and perhaps innocently spoken, may be carried by unknown currents and bring sorrow, misery and shame to the innocent. A cruel smile, a shrug of the shoulders or a cleverly eloquent silence may ruin in a moment the reputation a man or woman has been building for years.

It is as a single motion of the hand may destroy the delicate geometry of a spider's web, spun from its own body and life, though all the united efforts of the universe could not put it back as it was.

We do not need to judge nearly so much as we think we do. This is the age of snap judgments. The habit is greatly intensified by the sensational press. Twenty-four hours after a great murder there is difficulty in getting enough men who have not already formulated a judgment, to try the case. These men, in most instances, have read and accepted the garbled, highly colored newspaper account; they have to their own satisfaction discovered the murderer, practically tried him and—sentenced him. We hear readers state their decisions with all the force and absoluteness of one who has had the whole Book of Life made luminant and spread out before him. If there be one place in life where the attitude of the agnostic is beautiful, it is in this matter of judging others. It is the courage to say: "I don't know. I am waiting further evidence. I must hear both sides of the question. Till then I suspend all judgment." It is this suspended judgment that is the supreme form of charity.

It is strange that in life we recognize the right of every criminal to have a fair, open trial, yet we condemn unheard the dear friends around us on mere circumstantial evidence. We rely on the mere evidence of our senses, trust it implicitly, and permit it to sweep away like a mighty tide the faith that has been ours for years. We see all life grow dark, hope sink before our eyes, and the golden treasures of memory turn to cruel thoughts of loss to sting us with maddening pain. Our hasty judgment, that a few moments of explanation would remove, has estranged the friend of our life. If we be thus unjust to those we hold dear, what must be the cruel injustice of our judgment of others?

We know nothing of the trials, sorrows and temptations of those around us, of pillows wet with sobs, of the life-tragedy that may be hidden behind a smile, of the secret cares, struggles and worries that shorten life and leave their mark in hair prematurely whitened, and in character changed and almost re-created in a few days.

We say sometimes to one who seems calm and smiling: "You ought to be supremely happy; you have everything that heart could wish." It may be that at that very moment the person is passing alone through some agony of sorrow, where the teeth seem almost to bite into the lips in the attempt to keep feelings under control, when life seems a living death from which there is no relief. Then these light, flippant phrases jar upon us, and we seem as isolated and separated from the rest of humanity as if we were living on another planet.

Let us not dare to add to the burden of another the pain of our judgment. If we would guard our lips from expressing, we must control our mind, we must stop this continual sitting in judgment on the acts of others, even in private. Let us by daily exercises in self-control learn to turn off the process of judging—as we would turn off the gas. Let us eliminate pride, passion, personal feeling, prejudice and pettiness from our mind, and higher, purer emotions will rush in, as air seeks to fill a vacuum. Charity is not a formula; it is an atmosphere. Let us cultivate charity in judging; let us seek to draw out latent good in others rather than to discover hidden evil. It requires the eye of charity to see the undeveloped butterfly in the caterpillar. Let us, if we would rise to the full glory of our privilege, to the dignity of true living, make for our watchword the injunction of the supreme charity of the world—"Judge not."

V

Worry, *the* Great American Disease

WORRY is the most popular form of suicide. Worry impairs appetite, disturbs sleep, makes respiration irregular, spoils digestion, irritates disposition, warps character, weakens mind, stimulates disease, and saps bodily health. It is the real cause of death in thousands of instances where some other disease is named in the death certificate. Worry is mental poison; work is mental food.

When a child's absorption in his studies keeps him from sleeping, or when he tosses and turns from side to side, muttering the multiplication table or spelling words aloud, when sleep does come, then that child shows he is worrying. It is one of Nature's danger-signals raised to warn parents, and in mercy the parent should take a firm stand. The burden of that child's daily tasks should be lightened, the tension of its concentration should be lessened, the hours of its slavery to education should be cut short.

When a man or woman works over in dreams the problems of the day, when the sleeping hours are spent in turning the kaleidoscope of the day's activities, then there is either overwork or worry, and most likely it is the worry that comes from overwork. The Creator never intended a healthy mind to dream of the day's duties. Either dreamless sleep or dreams of the past should be the order of the night.

When the spectre of one grief, one fear, one sorrow, obtrudes itself between the eye and the printed page; when the inner voice of this irritating memory, or fear, looms up so loud as to deaden outside voices, there is danger to the individual. When all day, every hour, every moment, there is the dull, insistent, numb pain of something that makes itself felt through, above and below all our other thinking, we must know that we are worrying. Then there is but one thing to do,—we must stop that worry; we must kill it.

The wise men of this wondrous century have made great discoveries in their interviews with Nature. They have discovered that everything that has been created has its uses. They will teach you not to assassinate flies with paper coated with sweetened glue, for "the flies are Nature's scavengers." They will tell you just what are the special duties and responsibilities of each of the microscopic microbes with telescopic names. In their wildest moods of scientific enthusiasm they may venture to persuade you into believing that even the *mosquito* serves some real purpose in Nature, but no man that has ever lived can truthfully say a good word about worry.

Worry is forethought gone to seed. Worry is discounting possible future sorrows so that the individual may have present misery. Worry is the father of insomnia. Worry is the traitor in our camp that dampens our powder, weakens our aim. Under the guise of helping us to bear the present, and to be ready for the future, worry multiplies enemies within our own mind to sap our strength.

Worry is the dominance of the mind by a single vague, restless, unsatisfied, fearing and fearful idea. The mental energy and force that should be concentrated on the successive duties of the day is constantly and surreptitiously abstracted and absorbed by this one fixed idea. The full rich strength of the *unconscious* working of the mind, that which produces our best success, that represents our finest activity, is tapped, led away and wasted on worry.

Worry must not be confused with anxiety, though both words agree in meaning, originally, a "choking," or a "strangling," referring, of course, to the throttling effect upon individual activity. Anxiety faces large issues of life seriously, calmly, with dignity. Anxiety always suggests hopeful possibility; it is active in being ready, and devising measures to meet the outcome.

Worry is not one large individual sorrow; it is a colony of petty, vague, insignificant, restless imps of fear, that become important only from their combination, their constancy, their iteration.

When Death comes, when the one we love has passed from us, and the silence and the loneness and the emptiness of all things make us stare dry-eyed into the future, we give ourselves up, for a time, to the agony of isolation. This is not a petty worry we must kill ere it kills us. This is the awful majesty of sorrow that mercifully benumbs us, though it may later become, in the mysterious working of omnipotence, a rebaptism and a regeneration. It is the worry *habit*, the constant magnifying of petty sorrows to eclipse the sun of happiness, against which I here make protest.

To cure worry, the individual must be his own physician; he must give the case heroic treatment. He must realize, with every fibre of his being, the utter, absolute uselessness of worry. He must not think this is commonplace,—a bit of mere theory; it is a reality that he must translate for himself from mere words to a real, living fact. He must fully understand that if it were possible for him to spend a whole series of eternities in worry, it would not change the fact one jot or tittle. It is a time for action, not worry, because worry paralyzes thought and action, too. If you set down a column of figures in addition, no amount of worry can change the sum total of those figures. That result is wrapped up in the inevitability of mathematics. The result can be made different only by changing the figures as they are set down, one by one, in that column.

The one time that a man cannot afford to worry is when he *does* worry. Then he is facing, or imagines he is, a critical turn in affairs. This is the time when he needs one hundred per cent, of his mental energy to make his plans quickly, to see what is his wisest decision, to keep a clear eye on the sky and on his course, and a firm hand on the helm until he has weathered the storm in safety.

There are two reasons why man should not worry, either one of which must operate in every instance. First, because he *cannot* prevent the results he fears. Second, because he *can* prevent them. If he be powerless to avert the blow, he needs perfect mental concentration to meet it bravely, to lighten its force, to get what salvage he can from the wreck, to sustain his strength at this time when he must plan a new future. If he *can* prevent the evil he fears, then he has no need to worry, for he would by so doing be dissipating energy in his very hour of need.

If man do, day by day, ever the best he can by the light he has, he has no need to fear, no need to regret, no need to worry. No agony of worry would do aught to help him. Neither mortal nor angel can do more than his best.

If we look back upon our past life we will see how, in the marvellous working of events, the cities of our greatest happiness and of our fullest success have been built along the rivers of our deepest sorrows, our most abject failures. We then realize that our present happiness or success would have been impossible had it not been for some terrible affliction or loss in the past,—some wondrous potent force in the evolution of our character or our fortune. This should be a wondrous stimulus to us in bearing the trials and sorrows of life.

To cure one's self of worry is not an easy task; it is not to be removed in two or three applications of the quack medicine of any cheap philosophy, but it requires only clear, simple common-sense applied to the business of life. Man has no right to waste his own energies, to weaken his own powers and influence, for he has inalienable duties to himself, to his family, to society, and to the world.

VI

The Greatness *of* Simplicity

SIMPLICITY is the elimination of the non-essential in all things. It reduces life to its minimum of real needs; raises it to its maximum of powers. Simplicity means the survival,—not of the fittest, but of the best. In morals it kills the weeds of vice and weakness so that the flowers of virtue and strength may have room to grow. Simplicity cuts off waste and intensifies concentration. It converts flickering torches into searchlights.

All great truths are simple. The essence of Christianity could be given in a few words; a lifetime would be but continued seeking to make those words real and living in thoughts and acts. The true Christian's individual belief is always simpler than his church creed, and upon these vital, foundation elements he builds his life. Higher criticism never rises to the heights of his simplicity. He does not care whether the whale swallowed Jonah or Jonah swallowed the whale. Hair-splitting interpretation of words and phrases is an intellectual dissipation he has no time for. He cares naught for the anatomy of religion; he has its soul. His simple faith he lives,—in thought and word and act, day by day. Like the lark he lives nearest the ground; like the lark he soars highest toward heaven.

The minister whose sermons are made up merely of flowers of rhetoric, sprigs of quotation, sweet fancy, and perfumed commonplaces, is—consciously or unconsciously—posing in the pulpit. His literary charlotte-russes, sweet froth on a spongy, pulpy base, never helped a human soul,—they give neither strength nor inspiration. If the mind and heart of the preacher were really thrilled with the greatness and simplicity of religion, he would, week by week, apply the ringing truths of his faith to the vital problems of daily living. The test of a strong, simple sermon is results,—not the Sunday praise of his auditors, but their bettered lives during the week. People who pray on their knees on Sunday and prey on their neighbors on Monday, need simplicity in their faith.

No character can be simple unless it is based on truth—unless it is lived in harmony with one's own conscience and ideals. Simplicity is the pure white light of a life lived from within. It is destroyed by any attempt to live in harmony with public opinion. Public opinion is a conscience owned by a syndicate,—where the individual is merely a stockholder. But the individual has a conscience of which he is sole proprietor. Adjusting his life to his own ideals is the royal road to simplicity. Affectation is the confession of inferiority; it is an unnecessary proclamation that one is not living the life he pretends to live.

Simplicity is restful contempt for the non-essentials of life. It is restless hunger for the non-essentials that is the secret of most of the discontent of the world. It is constant striving to outshine others that kills simplicity and happiness.

Nature, in all her revelations, seeks to teach man the greatness of simplicity. Health is but the living of a physical life in harmony with a few simple, clearly defined laws. Simple food, simple exercise, simple precautions will work wonders. But man grows tired of the simple things, he yields to subtle temptations in eating and drinking, listens to his palate instead of to Nature,—and he suffers. He is then led into intimate acquaintance with dyspepsia, and he sits like a child at his own bounteous table, forced to limit his eating to simple food that he scorned.

There is a tonic strength, in the hour of sorrow and affliction, in escaping from the world and society and getting back to the simple duties and interests we have slighted and forgotten. Our world grows smaller, but it grows dearer and greater. Simple things have a new charm for us, and we suddenly realize that we have been renouncing all that is greatest and best, in our pursuit of some phantom.

Simplicity is the characteristic that is most difficult to simulate. The signature that is most difficult to imitate is the one that is most simple, most individual and most free from flourishes. The bank note that is the most difficult to counterfeit successfully is the one that contains the fewest lines and has the least intricate detail. So simple is it that any departure from the normal is instantly apparent. So is it also in mind and in morals.

Simplicity in act is the outward expression of simplicity in thought. Men who carry on their shoulders the fate of a nation are quiet, modest, unassuming. They are often made gentle, calm and simple by the discipline of their responsibility. They have no room in their minds for the pettiness of personal vanity. It is ever the drum-major who grows pompous when he thinks that the whole world is watching him as he marches at the head of the procession. The great general, bowed with the honors of many campaigns, is simple and unaffected as a child.

The college graduate assumes the airs of one to whom is committed the wisdom of the ages, while the great man of science, the Columbus of some great continent of investigation, is simple and humble.

The longest Latin derivatives seem necessary to express the thoughts of young writers. The world's great masters in literature can move mankind to tears, give light and life to thousands in darkness and doubt, or scourge a nation for its folly,—by words so simple as to be commonplace. But transfigured by the divinity of genius, there seems almost a miracle in words.

Life grows wondrously beautiful when we look at it as simple, when we can brush aside the trivial cares and sorrows and worries and failures and say: "They don't count. They are not the real things of life; they are but interruptions. There is something within me, my individuality, that makes all these gnats of trouble seem too trifling for me to permit them to have any dominion over me." Simplicity is a mental soil where artifice, lying, deceit, treachery and selfish, low ambition,—cannot grow.

The man whose character is simple looks truth and honesty so straight in the face that he has no consciousness of intrigue and corruption around him. He is deaf to the hints and whispers of wrongs that a suspicious nature would suspect even before they existed. He scorns to meet intrigue with intrigue, to hold power by bribery, to pay weak tribute to an inferior that has a temporary inning. To true simplicity, to perceive a truth is to begin to live it, to see a duty is to begin to do it. Nothing great can ever enter into the consciousness of a man of simplicity and remain but a theory. Simplicity in a character is like the needle of a compass,—it knows only one point, its North, its ideal.

Let us seek to cultivate this simplicity in all things in our life. The first step toward simplicity is "simplifying." The beginning of mental or moral progress or reform is always renunciation or sacrifice. It is rejection, surrender or destruction of separate phases of habit or life that have kept us from higher things. Reform your diet and you simplify it; make your speech truer and higher and you simplify it; reform your morals and you begin to cut off your immorals. The secret of all true greatness is simplicity. Make simplicity the keynote of your life and you will be great, no matter though your life be humble and your influence seem but little. Simple habits, simple manners, simple needs, simple words, simple faiths,—all are the pure manifestations of a mind and heart of simplicity.

Simplicity is never to be associated with weakness and ignorance. It means reducing tons of ore to nuggets of gold. It means the light of fullest knowledge; it means that the individual has seen the folly and the nothingness of those things that make up the sum of the life of others. He has lived *down* what others are blindly seeking to live *up* to. Simplicity is the sun of a self-centred and pure life,—the secret of any specific greatness in the life of the individual.

VII

Living Life Over Again

DURING a terrific storm a few years ago a ship was driven far out of her course, and, helpless and disabled, was carried into a strange bay. The water supply gave out, and the crew suffered the agony of thirst, yet dared not drink of the salt water in which their vessel floated. In the last extremity they lowered a bucket over the ship's side, and in desperation quaffed the beverage they thought was sea-water. But to their joy and amazement the water was fresh, cool and life-giving. They were in a fresh-water arm of the sea, and they did not know it. They had simply to reach down and accept the new life and strength for which they prayed.

Man, to-day, heart-weary with the sorrow, sin and failure of his past life, feels that he could live a better life if he could only have another chance, if he could only live life over again, if he could only start afresh with his present knowledge and experience. He looks back with regretful memory to the golden days of youth and sadly mourns his wasted chances. He then turns hopefully to the thought of a life to come. But, helpless, he stands between the two ends of life, yet thirsting for the chance to live a new life, according to his bettered condition for living it. In his blindness and unknowing, he does not realize, like the storm-driven sailors, that the new life is all around him; he has but to reach out and take it. Every day is a new life, every sunrise but a new birth for himself and the world, every morning the beginning of a new existence for him, a new, great chance to put to new and higher uses the results of his past living.

The man who looks back upon his past life and says, "I have nothing to regret," has lived in vain. The life without regret is the life without gain. Regret is but the light of fuller wisdom, from our past, illumining our future. It means that we are wiser today than we were yesterday. This new wisdom means new responsibility, new privileges; it is a new chance for a better life. But if regret remain merely "regret," it is useless; it must become the revelation of new possibilities, and the inspiration and source of strength to realize them. Even omnipotence could not change the past, but each man, to a degree far beyond his knowing, holds his future in his own hands.

If man were sincere in his longing to live life over he would get more help from his failures. If he realize his wasted golden hours of opportunity, let him not waste other hours in useless regret, but seek to forget his folly and to keep before him only the lessons of it. His past extravagance of time should lead him to minify his loss by marvellous economy of present

41

moments. If his whole life be darkened by the memory of a cruel wrong he has done another, if direct amends be impossible to the injured one, passed from life, let him make the world the legatee to receive his expressions of restitution. Let his regret and sorrow be manifest in words of kindness and sympathy, and acts of sweetness and love given to all with whom he comes in contact. If he regrets a war he has made against one individual, let him place the entire world on his pension list. If a man make a certain mistake once, the only way he can properly express his recognition of it is not to make a similar mistake later. Josh Billings once said: "A man who is bitten twice by the same dog is better adapted to that business than any other."

There are many people in this world who want to live life over because they take such pride in their past. They resemble the beggars in the street who tell you they "have seen better days." It is not what man *was* that shows character; it is what he progressively *is*. Trying to obtain a present record on a dead past is like some present-day mediocrity that tries to live on its ancestry. We look for the fruit in the branches of the family tree, not in the roots. Showing how a family degenerated from a noble ancestor of generations ago to its present representative is not a boast;—it is an unnecessary confession. Let man think less of his own ancestors and more of those he is preparing for his posterity; less of his past virtue, and more of his future.

When man pleads for a chance to live life over, there is always an implied plea of inexperience, of a lack of knowledge. This is unworthy, even of a coward. We know the laws of health, yet we ignore them or defy them every day. We know what is the proper food for us, individually, to eat, yet we gratify our appetites and trust to our cleverness to square the account with Nature somehow. We know that success is a matter of simple, clearly defined laws, of the development of mental essentials, of tireless energy and concentration, of constant payment of price,—we know all this, and yet we do not live up to our knowledge. We constantly eclipse ourselves by ourselves, and then we blame Fate.

Parents often counsel their children against certain things, and do them themselves, in the foolish hope that the children will believe their ears in preference to their eyes. Years of careful teaching of a child to be honest and truthful may be nullified in an instant by a parent's lying to a conductor about a child's age to save a nickel. That may be a very expensive street-car ride for the child,—and for the parent. It may be part of the spirit of the age to believe that it is no sin to cheat a corporation or a trust, but it is unwise to give the child so striking an example at an age when it cannot detect the sophistry.

Man's only plea for a chance to live life again is that he has gained in wisdom and experience. If he be really in earnest, then he can live life over, he can live life anew, he can live the new life that comes to him day by day. Let him leave to the past, to the aggregated thousands of yesterdays, all their mistakes, sin, sorrow, misery and folly, and start afresh. Let him close the books of his old life, let him strike a balance, and start anew, crediting himself with all the wisdom he has gained from his past failure and weakness, and charging himself with the new duties and responsibilities that come from the possession of his new capital of wisdom. Let him criticise others less and himself more,—and start out bravely in this new life he is to live.

What the world needs is more day-to-day living; starting in the morning with fresh, clear ideals for that day, and seeking to live that day, and each successive hour and moment of that day, as if it were all time and all eternity. This has in it no element of disregard for the future, for each day is set in harmony with that future. It is like the sea-captain heading his vessel toward his port of destination, and day by day keeping her steaming toward it. This view of living kills morbid regret of the past, and morbid worry about the future. Most people want large, guaranteed slices of life; they would not be satisfied with manna fresh every day, as was given to the children of Israel; they want grain elevators filled with daily bread.

Life is worth living if it be lived in a way that is worth living. Man does not own his life,—to do with as he will. He has merely a life-interest in it. He must finally surrender it,—with an accounting. At each New Year tide it is common to make new resolutions, but in the true life of the individual each day is the beginning of a New Year if he will only make it so. A mere date on the calendar of eternity is no more a divider of time than a particular grain of sand divides the desert.

Let us not make heroic resolutions so far beyond our strength that the resolution becomes a dead memory within a week; but let us promise ourselves that each day will be the new beginning of a newer, better and truer life for ourselves, for those around us, and for the world.

VIII

Syndicating Our Sorrows

THE most selfish man in the world is the one who is most unselfish,—with his sorrows. He does not leave a single misery of his untold to you, or unsuffered by you,—he gives you all of them. The world becomes to him a syndicate formed to take stock in his private cares, worries and trials. His mistake is in forming a syndicate; he should organize a trust and control it all himself, then he could keep everyone from getting any of his misery.

Life is a great, serious problem for the individual. All our greatest joys and our deepest sorrows come to us,—alone. We must go into our Gethsemane,—alone. We must battle against the mighty weakness within us,—alone. We must live our own life,—alone. We must die,—alone. We must accept the full responsibility of our life,—alone. If each one of us has this mighty problem of life to solve for himself, if each of us has his own cares, responsibilities, failures, doubts, fears, bereavements, we surely are playing a coward's part when we syndicate our sorrows to others.

We should seek to make life brighter for others; we should

seek to hearten them in their trials by the example of our courage in bearing our sorrows. We should seek to forget our failures, and remember only the new wisdom they gave us; we should live down our griefs by counting the joys and privileges still left to us; put behind us our worries and regrets, and face each new day of life as bravely as we can. But we have no right to retail our sorrow and unhappiness through the community.

Autobiography constitutes a large part of the conversation of some people. It is not really conversation,—it is an uninterrupted monologue. These people study their individual lives with a microscope, and then they throw an enlarged view of their miseries on a screen and lecture on them, as a stereopticon man discourses on the microbes in a drop of water. They tell you that "they did not sleep a wink all night; they heard the clock strike every quarter of an hour." Now, there is no real cause for thus boasting of insomnia. It requires no peculiar talent,—even though it does come only to wide-awake people.

If you ask such a man how he is feeling, he will trace the whole genealogy of his present condition down from the time he had the grippe four years ago. You hoped for a word; he gives you a treatise. You asked for a sentence; he delivers an encyclopedia. His motto is: "Every man his own Boswell." He is syndicating his sorrows.

The woman who makes her trials with her children, her

troubles with her servants, her difficulties with her family, the subjects of conversation with her callers is syndicating her sorrows. If she has a dear little innocent child who recites "Curfew Shall Not Ring Tonight," is it not wiser for the mother to bear it calmly and discreetly and in silence, than to syndicate this sorrow?

The business man who lets his dyspepsia get into his disposition, and who makes everyone around him suffer because he himself is ill, is syndicating ill-health. We have no right to make others the victims of our moods. If illness makes us cross and irritable, makes us unjust to faithful workers who cannot protest, let us quarantine ourselves so that we do not spread the contagion. Let us force ourselves to speak slowly, to keep anger away from the eyes, to prevent temper showing in the voice. If we feel that we *must* have dyspepsia, let us keep it out of our head, let us keep it from getting north of the neck.

Most people sympathize too much with themselves. They take themselves as a single sentence isolated from the great text of life. They study themselves too much as separated from the rest of humanity, instead of being vitally connected with their fellow-men. There are some people who surrender to sorrow as others give way to dissipation. There is a vain pride of sorrow as well as of beauty. Most individuals have a strange glow of vanity in looking back upon their past and feeling that few others in life have suffered such trials, hardships and disappointments as have come to them.

When Death comes into the little circle of loved ones who make up our world, all life becomes dark to us. We seem to have no reason for existing, no object, no incentive, no hope. The love that made struggle and effort bearable for us,—is gone. We stare, dry-eyed, into the future, and see no future; we want none. Life has become to us a past,—with no future. It is but a memory, without a hope.

Then in the divine mystery of Nature's processes, under the tender, soothing touch of Time, as days melt into weeks, we begin to open our eyes gently to the world around us, and the noise and tumult of life jars less and less upon us. We have become emotionally convalescent. As the days go on, in our deep love, in the fullness of our loyalty, we protest often, with tears in our eyes, against our gradual return to the spirit and atmosphere of the days of the past. We feel in a subtle way a new pain, as if we were disloyal to the dear one, as if we were faithless to our love. Nature sweetly turns aside our protesting hands, and says to us, "There is no disloyalty in permitting the wounds to lessen their pain, to heal gradually, if Time foreordain that they can heal." There are some natures, all-absorbed in a mighty love, wherein no healing is possible,— but these are rare souls in life.

Bitter though our anguish be, we have no right to syndicate our sorrow. We have no right to cast a gloom over happy natures by our heavy weight of crape, by serving the term prescribed by Society for wearing the livery of mourning,—as if real grief thought of a uniform. We have no right to syndicate our grief by using notepaper with a heavy black border as wide as a hat-band, thus parading our personal sorrow to others in their happiest moments.

If life has not gone well with us, if fortune has left us disconsolate, if love has grown cold, and we sit alone by the embers; if life has become to us a valley of desolation, through which weary limbs must drag an unwilling body till the end shall come,—let us not radiate such an atmosphere to those round us; let us not take strangers through the catacombs of our life, and show the bones of our dead past; let us not pass our cup of sorrow to others, but, if we must drink it, let us take it as Socrates did his poison hemlock,—grandly, heroically and uncomplainingly.

If your life has led you to doubt the existence of honor in man and virtue in woman; if you feel that religion is a pretense, that spirituality is a sham, that life is a failure, and death the entrance to nothingness; if you have absorbed all the poison philosophy of the world's pessimists, and committed the folly of believing it,—don't syndicate it.

If your fellow-man be clinging to one frail spar, the last remnant of a noble, shipwrecked faith in God and humanity, let him keep it. Do not loosen his fingers from his hope, and tell him it is a delusion. How do you know? Who told you it was so?

If these high-tide moments of life sweep your faith in Omnipotence into nothingness, if the friend in whom you have put all faith in humanity and humanity's God betray you, do not eagerly accept the teachings of those modern freethinkers who syndicate their infidelity at so much per reserved seat. Seek to recover your lost faith by listening to the million voices that speak of infinite wisdom, infinite love, that manifest themselves in nature and humanity, and then build up as rapidly as you can a new faith, a faith in something higher, better and truer than you have known before.

You may have *one* in the world to whom you may dare show with the fullness of absolute confidence and perfect faith any thought, any hope, any sorrow,—but you dare not trust them to the world. Do not show the world through your Bluebeard chamber; keep your trials and sorrows as close to you as you can till you have mastered them. Don't weaken others by thus—syndicating your miseries.

IX

The Revelations *of* Reserve Power

EVERY individual is a marvel of unknown and unrealized possibilities. Nine-tenths of an iceberg is always below water. Nine-tenths of the possibilities of good and evil of the individual is ever hidden from his sight.

Burns' prayer,—that we might "see oursels as ithers see us,"—was weak. The answer could minister only to man's vanity,—it would show him only what others think him to be, not what he is. We should pray to see ourselves as we *are*. But no man could face the radiant revelation of the latent powers and forces within him, underlying the weak, narrow life he is living. He would fall blinded and prostrate as did Moses before the burning bush. Man is not a mechanical music-box wound up by the Creator and set to play a fixed number of prescribed tunes. He is a human harp, with infinite possibilities of unawakened music.

The untold revelations of Nature are in her Reserve Power. Reserve Power is Nature's method of meeting emergencies. Nature is wise and economic. Nature saves energy and effort, and gives only what is absolutely necessary for life and development under any given condition, and when new needs arise Nature always meets them by her Reserve Power.

In animal life Nature reveals this in a million phases. Animals placed in the darkness of the Mammoth Cave gradually have the sense of sight weakened and the senses of smell, touch and hearing intensified. Nature watches over all animals, making their color harmonize with the general tone of their surroundings to protect them from their enemies. Those arctic animals which in the summer inhabit regions free from snow, turn white when winter comes. In the desert, the lion, the camel and all the desert antelopes have more or less the color of the sand and rocks among which they live. In tropical forests parrots are usually green; turacous, barbets and bee-eaters have a preponderance of green in their plumage. The colors change as the habits of the animals change from generation to generation. Nature, by her Reserve Power, always meets the new needs of animals with new strength,— new harmony with new conditions.

About forty-five years ago three pairs of enterprising rabbits were introduced into Australia. To-day, the increase of these six immigrants may be counted by millions. They became a pest to the country. Fortunes have been spent to exterminate them. Wire fences many feet high and thousands of miles long have been built to keep out the invaders. The rabbits had to fight awful odds to live, but they have now outwitted man. They have developed a new nail,—a long nail by which they can retain their hold on the fence while climbing. With this same nail they can burrow six or eight inches under the netting, and thus enter the fields that mean food and life to them. They are now laughing at man. Reserve Power has vitalized for these rabbits latent possibilities because they did not tamely accept their condition, but in their struggle to live learned *how* to live.

In plant life, Nature is constantly revealing Reserve Power. The possibilities of almost infinite color are present in *every* green plant, even in roots and stems. Proper conditions only are needed to reveal them. By obeying Nature's laws man could make leaves as beautifully colored as flowers. The *wild* rose has only a single corolla; but, when cultivated in rich soil, the numerous yellow stamens change into the brilliant red leaves of the full-grown cabbage-rose. This is but one of Nature's miracles of Reserve Power. Once the banana was a tropical lily; the peach was at one time a bitter almond. To tell the full story of Reserve Power in Nature would mean to write the history of the universe, in a thousand volumes.

Nature is a great believer in "double engines." Man is equipped with nearly every organ in duplicate—eyes, ears, lungs, arms and legs, so that if one be weakened, its mate, through Reserve Power, is stimulated to do enough for both. Even where the organ itself is not duplicated, as in the nose, there is a division of parts so there is constant reserve. Nature, for still further protection, has for every part of the body an understudy in training, to be ready in a crisis,—as the sense of touch for the blind.

Birds when frightened ruffle their feathers; a dog that has been in the water shakes its coat so that each hair stands out of itself; the startled hedgehog projects every quill. These actions are produced by "skin muscles" that are rudimentary in man, and over which in ordinary conditions he has no control. But in a moment of terrible fear Reserve Power quickens their action in a second, and the hair on his head "stands on end" in the intensity of his fright.

Nature, that thus watches so tenderly over the physical needs of man, is equally provident in storing for him a mental and a moral Reserve Power. Man may fail in a dozen different lines of activity and then succeed brilliantly in a phase wherein he was unconscious of any ability. We must never rest content with what we *are*, and say: "There is no use for me to try. I can never be great. I am not even clever now." But the law of Reserve Power stands by us as a fairy godmother and says: "There is one charm by which you can transmute the dull dross of your present condition into the pure gold of strength and power,—that charm is ever doing your best, ever daring more, and the full measure of your final attainment can never be told in advance. Rely upon me to help you with new revelations of strength in new emergencies. Never be cast down because your power seems so trifling, your progress so slow. The world's greatest and best men were failures in some line, failures many times before failure was crowned with success."

There is in the mythology of the Norsemen a belief that the strength of an enemy we kill enters into us. This is true in character. As we conquer a passion, a thought, a feeling, a desire; as we rise superior to some impulse, the strength of that victory, trifling though it may be, is stored by Nature as a Reserve Power to come to us in the hour of our need.

Were we to place before almost any individual the full chart of his future,—his trials, sorrows, failures, afflictions, loss, sickness and loneliness,—and ask him if he could bear it, he would say: "No! I could not bear all that and live." But he *can* and he *does*. The hopes upon the realization of which he has staked all his future turn to air as he nears them; friends whom he has trusted betray him; the world grows cold to him; the child whose smile is the light of his life dishonors his name; death takes from him the wife of his heart. Reserve Power has been watching over him and ever giving him new strength,—even while he sleeps.

If we be conscious of any weakness, and desire to conquer it, we can force ourselves into positions where we *must* act in a way to strengthen ourselves through that weakness, cut off our retreat, burn our bridges behind us, and fight like Spartans till the victory be ours.

Reserve Power is like the manna given to the children of Israel in the wilderness,—only enough was given them to keep them for one day. Each successive day had its new supply of strength. There is in the leaning tower of Pisa a spiral stairway so steep in its ascent that only one step at a time is revealed to us. But as each step is taken the next is made visible, and thus, step by step, to the very highest. So in the Divine economy of the universe, Reserve Power is a gradual and constant revelation of strength within us to meet each new need. And no matter what be our line of life, what our need, we should feel that we have within us infinite, untried strength and possibility, and that, if we believe and do our best, the Angel of Reserve Power will walk by our side, and will even divide the waters of the Red Sea of our sorrows and trials so we may walk through in safety.

X

The Majesty *of* Calmness

CALMNESS is the rarest quality in human life. It is the poise
of a great nature, in harmony with itself and its ideals. It is
the moral atmosphere of a life self-centred, self-reliant, and
self-controlled. Calmness is singleness of purpose, absolute
confidence, and conscious power,—ready to be focused in an
instant to meet any crisis.

The Sphinx is not a true type of calmness,—petrifaction
is not calmness; it is death, the silencing of all the energies;
while no one lives his life more fully, more intensely and more
consciously than the man who is calm.

The Fatalist is not calm. He is the coward slave of his
environment, hopelessly surrendering to his present condition,
recklessly indifferent to his future. He accepts his life as a
rudderless ship, drifting on the ocean of time. He has no
compass, no chart, no known port to which he is sailing. His
self-confessed inferiority to all nature is shown in his existence
of constant surrender. It is not,—calmness.

The man who is calm has his course in life clearly marked
on his chart. His hand is ever on the helm. Storm, fog, night,

tempest, danger, hidden reefs,—he is ever prepared and ready for them. He is made calm and serene by the realization that in these crises of his voyage he needs a clear mind and a cool head; that he has naught to do but to do each day the best he can by the light he has; that he will never flinch nor falter for a moment; that, though he may have to tack and leave his course for a time, he will never drift, he will get back into the true channel, he will keep ever headed toward his harbor. *When* he will reach it, *how* he will reach it matters not to him. He rests in calmness, knowing he has done his best. If his best seem to be overthrown or overruled, then he must still bow his head,—in calmness. To no man is permitted to know the future of his life, the finality. God commits to man ever only new beginnings, new wisdom, and new days to use to the best of his knowledge.

Calmness comes ever from within. It is the peace and restfulness of the depths of our nature. The fury of storm and of wind agitate only the surface of the sea; they can penetrate only two or three hundred feet,—below that is the calm, unruffled deep. To be ready for the great crises of life we must learn serenity in our daily living. Calmness is the crown of self-control.

When the worries and cares of the day fret you, and begin to wear upon you, and you chafe under the friction,—be calm. Stop, rest for a moment, and let calmness and peace assert themselves. If you let these irritating outside influences get the better of you, you are confessing your inferiority to them, by permitting them to dominate you. Study the disturbing elements, each by itself, bring all the will-power of your nature to bear upon them, and you will find that they will, one by one, melt into nothingness, like vapors fading before the sun. The glow of calmness that will then pervade your mind, the tingling sensation of an inflow of new strength, may be to you the beginning of the revelation of the supreme calmness that is possible for you. Then, in some great hour of your life, when you stand face to face with some awful trial, when the structure of your ambition and life-work crumbles in a moment, you will be brave. You can then fold your arms calmly, look out undismayed and undaunted upon the ashes of your hope, upon the wreck of what you have faithfully built, and with brave heart and unfaltering voice you may say: "So let it be,—I will build again."

When the tongue of malice and slander, the persecution of inferiority, tempts you for just a moment to retaliate, when for an instant you forget yourself so far as to hunger for revenge,—be calm. When the grey heron is pursued by its enemy, the eagle, it does not run to escape; it remains calm, takes a dignified stand, and waits quietly, facing the enemy unmoved. With the terrific force with which the eagle makes its attack, the boasted king of birds is often impaled and run through on the quiet, lance-like bill of the heron. The means that man takes to kill another's character becomes suicide of his own.

No man in the world ever attempted to wrong another without being injured in return,—someway, somehow, sometime. The only weapon of offence that Nature seems to recognize is the boomerang. Nature keeps her books admirably; she puts down every item, she closes all accounts finally, but she does not always balance them at the end of the month. To the man who is calm, revenge is so far beneath him that he cannot reach it,—even by stooping. When injured, he does not retaliate; he wraps around him the royal robes of Calmness, and he goes quietly on his way.

When the hand of Death touches the one we hold dearest, paralyzes our energy, and eclipses the sun of our life, the calmness that has been accumulating in long years becomes in a moment our refuge, our reserve strength.

The most subtle of all temptations is the *seeming* success of the wicked. It requires moral courage to see, without flinching, material prosperity coming to men who are dishonest; to see politicians rise into prominence, power and wealth by trickery and corruption; to see virtue in rags and vice in velvets; to see ignorance at a premium, and knowledge at a discount. To the man who is really calm these puzzles of life do not appeal. He is living his life as best he can; he is not worrying about the problems of justice, whose solution must be left to Omniscience to solve.

When man has developed the spirit of Calmness until

it becomes so absolutely part of him that his very presence radiates it, he has made great progress in life. Calmness cannot be acquired of itself and by itself; it must come as the culmination of a series of virtues. What the world needs and what individuals need is a higher standard of living, a great realizing sense of the privilege and dignity of life, a higher and nobler conception of individuality.

With this great sense of calmness permeating an individual, man becomes able to retire more into himself, away from the noise, the confusion and strife of the world, which come to his ears only as faint, far-off rumblings, or as the tumult of the life of a city heard only as a buzzing hum by the man in a balloon.

The man who is calm does not selfishly isolate himself from the world, for he is intensely interested in all that concerns the welfare of humanity. His calmness is but a Holy of Holies into which he can retire *from* the world to get strength to live *in* the world. He realizes that the full glory of individuality, the crowning of his self-control is,—the majesty of calmness

XI

Hurry, *the* Scourge *of* America

THE first sermon in the world was preached at the Creation. It was a Divine protest against Hurry. It was a Divine object lesson of perfect law, perfect plan, perfect order, perfect method. Six days of work carefully planned, scheduled and completed were followed by,—rest. Whether we accept the story as literal or as figurative, as the account of successive days or of ages comprising millions of years, matters little if we but learn the lesson.

Nature is very un-American. Nature never hurries. Every phase of her working shows plan, calmness, reliability, and the absence of hurry. Hurry always implies lack of definite method, confusion, impatience of slow growth. The Tower of Babel, the world's first sky-scraper, was a failure because of hurry. The workers mistook their arrogant ambition for inspiration. They had too many builders,—and no architect. They thought to make up the lack of a head by a superfluity of hands. This is a characteristic of Hurry. It seeks ever to make energy a substitute for a clearly defined plan,—the result is ever as hopeless as trying to transform a hobbyhorse into a real steed by brisk riding.

Hurry is a counterfeit of haste. Haste has an ideal, a distinct aim to be realized by the quickest, direct methods. Haste has a single compass upon which it relies for direction and in harmony with which its course is determined. Hurry says: "I must move faster. I will get three compasses; I will have them different; I will be guided by all of them. One of them will probably be right." Hurry never realizes that slow, careful foundation work is the quickest in the end.

Hurry has ruined more Americans than has any other word in the vocabulary of life. It is the scourge of America; and is both a cause and a result of our high-pressure civilization. Hurry adroitly assumes so many masquerades of disguise that its identity is not always recognized.

Hurry always pays the highest price for everything, and, usually the goods are not delivered. In the race for wealth men often sacrifice time, energy, health, home, happiness and honor,—everything that money cannot buy, the very things that money can never bring back. Hurry is a phantom of paradoxes. Business men, in their desire to provide for the future happiness of their family, often sacrifice the present happiness of wife and children on the altar of Hurry. They forget that their place in the home should be something greater than being merely "the man that pays the bills;" they expect consideration and thoughtfulness that they are not giving.

We hear too much of a wife's duties to a husband and too

little of the other side of the question. "The wife," they tell us, "should meet her husband with a smile and a kiss, should tactfully watch his moods and be ever sweetness and sunshine." Why this continual swinging of the censer of devotion to the man of business? Why should a woman have to look up with timid glance at the face of her husband, to "size up his mood?" Has not her day, too, been one of care, and responsibility, and watchfulness? Has not mother-love been working over perplexing problems and worries of home and of the training of the children that wifely love may make her seek to solve in secret? Is man, then, the weaker sex that he must be pampered and treated as tenderly as a boil trying to keep from contact with the world?

In their hurry to attain some ambition, to gratify the dream of a life, men often throw honor, truth, and generosity to the winds. Politicians dare to stand by and see a city poisoned with foul water until they "see where they come in" on a waterworks appropriation. If it be necessary to poison an army,—that, too, is but an incident in the hurry for wealth.

This is the Age of the Hothouse. The element of natural growth is pushed to one side and the hothouse and the force-pump are substituted. Nature looks on tolerantly as she says: "So far you may go, but no farther, my foolish children."

The educational system of to-day is a monumental institution dedicated to Hurry. The children are forced to go through a series of studies that sweep the circle of all human wisdom.

They are given everything that the ambitious ignorance of the age can force into their minds; they are taught everything but the essentials,—how to use their senses and how to think. Their minds become congested by a great mass of undigested facts, and still the cruel, barbarous forcing goes on. You watch it until it seems you cannot stand it a moment longer, and you instinctively put out your hand and say: "Stop! This modern slaughter of the Innocents must *not* go on!" Education smiles suavely, waves her hand complacently toward her thousands of knowledge-prisons over the country, and says: "Who are you that dares speak a word against our sacred school system?" Education is in a hurry. Because she fails in fifteen years to do what half the time should accomplish by better methods, she should not be too boastful. Incompetence is not always a reason for pride. And they hurry the children into a hundred text-books, then into ill-health, then into the colleges, then into a diploma, then into life,—with a dazed mind, untrained and unfitted for the real duties of living.

Hurry is the deathblow to calmness, to dignity, to poise. The old-time courtesy went out when the new-time hurry came in. Hurry is the father of dyspepsia. In the rush of our national life, the bolting of food has become a national vice. The words "Quick Lunches" might properly be placed on thousands of headstones in our cemeteries. Man forgets that he is the only animal that dines; the others merely feed. Why does he abrogate his right to dine and go to the end of the line with the mere feeders? His self-respecting stomach rebels, and expresses its indignation by indigestion. Then man has to go through life with a little bottle of pepsin tablets in his vest-pocket. He is but another victim to this craze for speed. Hurry means the breakdown of the nerves. It is the royal road to nervous prostration.

Everything that is great in life is the product of slow growth; the newer, and greater, and higher, and nobler the work, the slower is its growth, the surer is its lasting success. Mushrooms attain their full power in a night; oaks require decades. A fad lives its life in a few weeks; a philosophy lives through generations and centuries. If you are sure you are right, do not let the voice of the world, or of friends, or of family swerve you for a moment from your purpose. Accept slow growth if it must be slow, and know the results *must* come, as you would accept the long, lonely hours of the night,—with absolute assurance that the heavy-leaded moments *must* bring the morning.

Let us as individuals banish the word "Hurry" from our lives. Let us care for nothing so much that we would pay honor and self-respect as the price of hurrying it. Let us cultivate calmness, restfulness, poise, sweetness,—doing our best, bearing all things as bravely as we can; living our life undisturbed by the prosperity of the wicked or the malice of the envious. Let us not be impatient, chafing at delay, fretting over failure, wearying over results, and weakening under opposition. Let us ever turn our face toward the future with confidence and trust, with the calmness of a life in harmony with itself, true to its ideals, and slowly and constantly progressing toward their realization.

Let us see that cowardly word Hurry in all its most degenerating phases, let us see that it ever kills truth, loyalty, thoroughness; and let us determine that, day by day, we will seek more and more to substitute for it the calmness and repose of a true life, nobly lived.

XII

The Power *of* Personal Influence

THE only responsibility that a man cannot evade in this life is the one he thinks of least,—his personal influence. Man's conscious influence, when he is on dress-parade, when he is posing to impress those around him,—is woefully small. But his unconscious influence, the silent, subtle radiation of his personality, the effect of his words and acts, the trifles he never considers,—is tremendous. Every moment of life he is changing to a degree the life of the whole world. Every man has an atmosphere which is affecting every other. So silent and unconsciously is this influence working, that man may forget that it exists.

All the forces of Nature,—heat, light, electricity and gravitation,—are silent and invisible. We never *see* them; we only know that they exist by seeing the effects they produce. In all Nature the wonders of the "seen" are dwarfed into insignificance when compared with the majesty and glory of the "unseen."

The great sun itself does not supply enough heat and light to sustain animal and vegetable life on the earth. We are dependent for nearly half of our light and heat upon the stars, and the greater part of this supply of life-giving energy comes from *invisible* stars, millions of miles from the earth. In a thousand ways Nature constantly seeks to lead men to a keener and deeper realization of the power and wonder of the invisible.

Into the hands of every individual is given a marvellous power for good or for evil,—the silent, unconscious, unseen influence of his life. This is simply the constant radiation of what a man really *is*, not what he pretends to be. Every man, by his mere living, is radiating sympathy, or sorrow, or morbidness, or cynicism, or happiness, or hope, or any of a hundred other qualities. Life is a state of constant radiation and absorption; to exist is to radiate; to exist is to be the recipient of radiations.

There are men and women whose presence seems to radiate sunshine, cheer and optimism. You feel calmed and rested and restored in a moment to a new and stronger faith in humanity. There are others who focus in an instant all your latent distrust, morbidness and rebellion against life. Without knowing why, you chafe and fret in their presence. You lose your bearings on life and its problems. Your moral compass is disturbed and unsatisfactory. It is made untrue in an instant, as the magnetic needle of a ship is deflected when it passes near great mountains of iron ore.

There are men who float down the stream of life like

icebergs,—cold, reserved, unapproachable and self-contained. In their presence you involuntarily draw your wraps closer around you, as you wonder who left the door open. These refrigerated human beings have a most depressing influence on all those who fall under the spell of their radiated chilliness. But there are other natures, warm, helpful, genial, who are like the Gulf Stream, following their own course, flowing undaunted and undismayed in the ocean of colder waters. Their presence brings warmth and life and the glow of sunshine, the joyous, stimulating breath of spring.

There are men who are like malarious swamps,—poisonous, depressing and weakening by their very presence. They make heavy, oppressive and gloomy the atmosphere of their own homes; the sound of the children's play is stilled, the ripples of laughter are frozen by their presence. They go through life as if each day were a new big funeral, and they were always chief mourners. There are other men who seem like the ocean; they are constantly bracing, stimulating, giving new draughts of tonic life and strength by their very presence.

There are men who are insincere in heart, and that insincerity is radiated by their presence. They have a wondrous interest in your welfare,—when they need you. They put on a "property" smile so suddenly, when it serves their purpose, that it seems the smile must be connected with some electric button concealed in their clothes. Their voice has a simulated cordiality that long training may have made almost natural.

But they never play their part absolutely true, the mask *will* slip down sometimes; their cleverness cannot teach their eyes the look of sterling honesty; they may deceive some people, but they cannot deceive all. There is a subtle power of revelation which makes us say: "Well, I cannot explain how it is, but I know that man is not honest."

Man cannot escape for one moment from this radiation of his character, this constantly weakening or strengthening of others. He cannot evade the responsibility by saying it is an unconscious influence. He can *select* the qualities that he will permit to be radiated. He can cultivate sweetness, calmness, trust, generosity, truth, justice, loyalty, nobility,—make them vitally active in his character,—and by these qualities he will constantly affect the world.

Discouragement often comes to honest souls trying to live the best they can, in the thought that they are doing so little good in the world. Trifles unnoted by us may be links in the chain of some great purpose. In 1797, William Godwin wrote The Inquirer, a collection of revolutionary essays on morals and politics. This book influenced Thomas Malthus to write his Essay on Population, published in 1798. Malthus' book suggested to Charles Darwin a point of view upon which he devoted many years of his life, resulting, in 1859, in the publication of The Origin of Species,—the most influential book of the nineteenth century, a book that has revolutionized all science. These were but three links of influence extending over sixty years.

It might be possible to trace this genealogy of influence back from Godwin, through generation and generation, to the word or act of some shepherd in early Britain, watching his flock upon the hills, living his quiet life, and dying with the thought that he had done nothing to help the world.

Men and women have duties to others,—and duties to themselves. In justice to ourselves we should refuse to live in an atmosphere that keeps us from living our best. If the fault be in us, we should master it. If it be the personal influence of others that, like a noxious vapor, kills our best impulses, we should remove from that influence,—if we can *possibly* move without forsaking duties. If it be wrong to move, then we should take strong doses of moral quinine to counteract the malaria of influence. It is not what those around us *do* for us that counts,—it is what they *are* to us. We carry our houseplants from one window to another to give them the proper heat, light, air and moisture. Should we not be at least as careful of ourselves?

To make our influence felt we must live our faith, we must practice what we believe. A magnet does not attract iron, as iron. It must first convert the iron into another magnet before it can attract it. It is useless for a parent to try to teach gentleness to her children when she herself is cross and irritable. The child who is told to be truthful and who hears a parent lie cleverly to escape some little social unpleasantness is not going to cling very zealously to truth. The parent's words say "don't lie," the influence of the parent's life says "do lie."

No man can ever isolate himself to evade this constant power of influence, as no single corpuscle can rebel and escape from the general course of the blood. No individual is so insignificant as to be without influence. The changes in our varying moods are all recorded in the delicate barometers of the lives of others. We should ever let our influence filter through human love and sympathy. We should not be merely an influence,—we should be an inspiration. By our very presence we should be a tower of strength to the hungering human souls around us.

XIII

The Dignity *of* Self-Reliance

SELF-CONFIDENCE, without self-reliance, is as useless as a cooking recipe,—without food. Self-confidence sees the possibilities of the individual; self-reliance realizes them. Self-confidence sees the angel in the unhewn block of marble; self-reliance carves it out for himself.

The man who is self-reliant says ever: "No one can realize my possibilities for me, but me; no one can make me good or evil but myself." He works out his own salvation,—financially, socially, mentally, physically, and morally. Life is an individual problem that man must solve for himself. Nature accepts no vicarious sacrifice, no vicarious service. Nature never recognizes a proxy vote. She has nothing to do with middlemen,—she deals only with the individual. Nature is constantly seeking to show man that he is his own best friend, or his own worst enemy. Nature gives man the option on which he will be to himself.

All the athletic exercises in the world are of no value to the individual unless he compel those bars and dumb-bells to yield to him, in strength and muscle, the power for which he, himself, pays in time and effort. He can never develop his muscles by sending his valet to a gymnasium.

The medicine-chests of the world are powerless, in all the united efforts, to help the individual until he reach out and take for himself what is needed for his individual weakness.

All the religions of the world are but speculations in morals, mere theories of salvation, until the individual realize that he must save himself by relying on the law of truth, as he sees it, and living his life in harmony with it, as fully as he can. But religion is not a Pullman car, with soft-cushioned seats, where he has but to pay for his ticket,—and someone else does all the rest. In religion, as in all other great things, he is ever thrown back on his self-reliance. He should accept all helps, but,—he must live his own life. He should not feel that he is a mere passenger; he is the engineer, and the train is his life. We must rely on ourselves, live our own lives, or we merely drift through existence,—losing all that is best, all that is greatest, all that is divine.

All that others can do for us is to give us opportunity. We must ever be prepared for the opportunity when it comes, and to go after it and find it when it does not come, or that opportunity is to us,—nothing. Life is but a succession of opportunities. They are for good or evil,—as we make them.

Many of the alchemists of old felt that they lacked but one element; if they could obtain that one, they believed they could transmute the baser metals into pure gold. It is so in character. There are individuals with rare mental gifts, and delicate spiritual discernment who fail utterly in life because they lack the one element,—self-reliance. This would unite all their energies, and focus them into strength and power.

The man who is not self-reliant is weak, hesitating and doubting in all he does. He fears to take a decisive step, because he dreads failure, because he is waiting for someone to advise him or because he dare not act in accordance with his own best judgment. In his cowardice and his conceit he sees all his non-success due to others. He is "not appreciated," "not recognized," he is "kept down." He feels that in some subtle way "society is conspiring against him." He grows almost vain as he thinks that no one has had such poverty, such sorrow, such affliction, such failure as have come to him.

The man who is self-reliant seeks ever to discover and conquer the weakness within him that keeps him from the attainment of what he holds dearest; he seeks within himself the power to battle against all outside influences. He realizes that all the greatest men in history, in every phase of human effort, have been those who have had to fight against the odds of sickness, suffering, sorrow. To him, defeat is no more than passing through a tunnel is to a traveller,—he knows he must emerge again into the sunlight.

The nation that is strongest is the one that is most self-reliant, the one that contains within its boundaries all that its people need. If, with its ports all blockaded it has not within itself the necessities of life and the elements of its continual progress then,—it is weak, held by the enemy, and it is but a question of time till it must surrender. Its independence is in proportion to its self-reliance, to its power to sustain itself from within. What is true of nations is true of individuals. The history of nations is but the biography of individuals magnified, intensified, multiplied, and projected on the screen of the past. History is the biography of a nation; biography is the history of an individual. So it must be that the individual who is most strong in any trial, sorrow or need is he who can live from his inherent strength, who needs no scaffolding of commonplace sympathy to uphold him. He must ever be self-reliant.

The wealth and prosperity of ancient Rome, relying on her slaves to do the real work of the nation, proved the nation's downfall. The constant dependence on the captives of war to do the thousand details of life for them, killed self-reliance in the nation and in the individual. Then, through weakened self-reliance and the increased opportunity for idle, luxurious ease that came with it, Rome, a nation of fighters, became,—a nation of men more effeminate than women. As we depend on others to do those things we should do ourselves, our self-reliance weakens and our powers and our control of them becomes continuously less.

Man to be great must be self-reliant. Though he may not be so in all things, he must be self-reliant in the one in which he would be great. This self-reliance is not the self-sufficiency of conceit. It is daring to stand alone. Be an oak, not a vine. Be ready to give support, but do not crave it; do not be dependent on it. To develop your true self-reliance, you must see from the very beginning that life is a battle you must fight for yourself,—you must be your own soldier. You cannot buy a substitute, you cannot win a reprieve, you can never be placed on the retired list. The retired list of life is,—death. The world is busy with its own cares, sorrows and joys, and pays little heed to you. There is but one great password to success,—self-reliance.

If you would learn to converse, put yourself into positions where you *must* speak. If you would conquer your morbidness, mingle with the bright people around you, no matter how difficult it may be. If you desire the power that someone else possesses, do not envy his strength, and dissipate your energy by weakly wishing his force were yours. Emulate the process by which it became his, depend on your self-reliance, pay the price for it, and equal power may be yours. The individual must look upon himself as an investment of untold possibilities if rightly developed,—a mine whose resources can never be known but by going down into it and bringing out what is hidden.

Man can develop his self-reliance by seeking constantly to surpass himself. We try too much to surpass others. If we seek ever to surpass ourselves, we are moving on a uniform line of progress, that gives a harmonious unifying to our growth in all its parts. Daniel Morrell, at one time President of the Cambria Rail Works, that employed 7,000 men and made a rail famed throughout the world, was asked the secret of the great success of the works. "We have no secret," he said, "but this,—we always try to beat our last batch of rails." Competition is good, but it has its danger side. There is a tendency to sacrifice real worth to mere appearance, to have seeming rather than reality. But the true competition is the competition of the individual with himself,—his present seeking to excel his past. This means real growth from within. Self-reliance develops it, and it develops self-reliance. Let the individual feel thus as to his own progress and possibilities, and he can almost create his life as he will. Let him never fall down in despair at dangers and sorrows at a distance; they may be harmless, like Bunyan's stone lions, when he nears them.

The man who is self-reliant does not live in the shadow of someone else's greatness; he thinks for himself, depends on himself, and acts for himself. In throwing the individual thus back upon himself it is not shutting his eyes to the stimulus and light and new life that come with the warm pressure of the hand, the kindly word and sincere expressions of true friendship. But true friendship is rare; its great value is in a crisis,—like a lifeboat. Many a boasted friend has proved a leaking, worthless "lifeboat" when the storm of adversity might make him useful. In these great crises of life, man is strong only as he is strong from within, and the more he depends on himself the stronger will he become, and the more able will he be to help others in the hour of their need. His very life will be a constant help and a strength to others, as he becomes to them a living lesson of the dignity of self-reliance.

XIV

Failure *as a* Success

IT ofttimes requires heroic courage to face fruitless effort, to take up the broken strands of a life-work, to look bravely toward the future, and proceed undaunted on our way. But what, to our eyes, may seem hopeless failure is often but the dawning of a greater success. It may contain in its débris the foundation material of a mighty purpose, or the revelation of new and higher possibilities.

Some years ago, it was proposed to send logs from Canada to New York, by a new method. The ingenious plan of Mr. Joggins was to bind great logs together by cables and iron girders and to tow the cargo as a raft. When the novel craft neared New York and success seemed assured, a terrible storm arose. In the fury of the tempest, the iron bands snapped like icicles and the angry water scattered the logs far and wide. The chief of the Hydrographic Department at Washington heard of the failure of the experiment, and at once sent word to shipmasters the world over, urging them to watch carefully for these logs which he described; and to note the precise location of each in latitude and longitude and the time the observation was made. Hundreds of captains, sailing over the waters of the earth, noted the logs, in the Atlantic Ocean, in the Mediterranean, in the South Seas—for into all waters did these venturesome ones travel. Hundreds of reports were made, covering a period of weeks and months. These observations were then carefully collated, systematized and tabulated, and discoveries were made as to the course of ocean currents that otherwise would have been impossible. The loss of the Joggins raft was not a real failure, for it led to one of the great discoveries in modern marine geography and navigation.

In our superior knowledge we are disposed to speak in a patronizing tone of the follies of the alchemists of old. But their failure to transmute the baser metals into gold resulted in the birth of chemistry. They did not succeed in what they attempted, but they brought into vogue the natural processes of sublimation, filtration, distillation, and crystallization; they invented the alembic, the retort, the sand-bag, the water-bath and other valuable instruments. To them is due the discovery of antimony, sulphuric ether and phosphorus, the cupellation of gold and silver, the determining of the properties of saltpetre and its use in gunpowder, and the discovery of the distillation of essential oils. This was the success of failure, a wondrous process of Nature for the highest growth,—a mighty lesson of comfort, strength, and encouragement if man would only realize and accept it.

Many of our failures sweep us to greater heights of success than we ever hoped for in our wildest dreams. Life is a successive unfolding of success from failure. In discovering America Columbus failed absolutely. His ingenious reasoning and experiment led him to believe that by sailing westward he would reach India. Every redman in America carries in his name "Indian," the perpetuation of the memory of the failure of Columbus. The Genoese navigator did not reach India; the cargo of "souvenirs" he took back to Spain to show to Ferdinand and Isabella as proofs of his success, really attested his failure. But the discovery of America was a greater success than was any finding of a "back-door" to India.

When David Livingstone had supplemented his theological education by a medical course, he was ready to enter the missionary field. For over three years he had studied tirelessly, with all energies concentrated on one aim,—to spread the gospel in China. The hour came when he was ready to start out with noble enthusiasm for his chosen work, to consecrate himself and his life to his unselfish ambition. Then word came from China that the "opium war" would make it folly to attempt to enter the country. Disappointment and failure did not long daunt him; he offered himself as missionary to Africa,—and he was accepted. His glorious failure to reach China opened a whole continent to light and truth. His study proved an ideal preparation for his labors as physician, explorer, teacher and evangel in the wilds of Africa.

Business reverses and the failure of his partner threw upon the broad shoulders and the still broader honor and honesty of Sir Walter Scott a burden of responsibility that forced him to write. The failure spurred him to almost superhuman effort. The masterpieces of Scotch historic fiction that have thrilled, entertained and uplifted millions of his fellow-men are a glorious monument on the field of a seeming failure.

When Millet, the painter of the "Angelus" worked on his almost divine canvas, in which the very air seems pulsing with the regenerating essence of spiritual reverence, he was painting against time, he was antidoting sorrow, he was racing against death. His brush strokes, put on in the early morning hours before going to his menial duties as a railway porter, in the dusk like that perpetuated on his canvas,—meant strength, food and medicine for the dying wife he adored. The art failure that cast him into the depths of poverty unified with marvellous intensity all the finer elements of his nature. This rare spiritual unity, this purging of all the dross of triviality, as he passed through the furnace of poverty, trial, and sorrow, gave eloquence to his brush and enabled him to paint as never before,—as no prosperity would have made possible.

Failure is often the turning-point, the pivot of circumstance that swings us to higher levels. It may not be financial success, it may not be fame; it may be new draughts of spiritual, moral or mental inspiration that will change us for all the later years of our life. Life is not really what comes to us, but what we get from it.

Whether man has had wealth or poverty, failure or success, counts for little when it is past. There is but one question for him to answer, to face boldly and honestly as an individual alone with his conscience and his destiny:

"How will I let that poverty or wealth affect me? If that trial or deprivation has left me better, truer, nobler, then,—poverty has been riches, failure has been a success. If wealth has come to me and has made me vain, arrogant, contemptuous, uncharitable, cynical, closing from me all the tenderness of life, all the channels of higher development, of possible good to my fellow-man, making me the mere custodian of a money-bag, then,—wealth has lied to me, it has been failure, not success; it has not been riches, it has been dark, treacherous poverty that stole from me even Myself." All things become for us then what we take from them.

Failure is one of God's educators. It is experience leading man to higher things; it is the revelation of a way, a path hitherto unknown to us. The best men in the world, those who have made the greatest real successes look back with serene happiness on their failures. The turning of the face of Time shows all things in a wondrously illuminated and satisfying perspective.

Many a man is thankful to-day that some petty success for which he once struggled, melted into thin air as his hand sought to clutch it. Failure is often the rock-bottom foundation of real success. If man, in a few instances of his life can say, "Those failures were the best things in the world that could have happened to me," should he not face new failures with undaunted courage and trust that the miraculous ministry of Nature may transform these new stumbling-blocks into new stepping-stones?

Our highest hopes are often destroyed to prepare us for better things. The failure of the caterpillar is the birth of the butterfly; the passing of the bud is the becoming of the rose; the death or destruction of the seed is the prelude to its resurrection as wheat. It is at night, in the darkest hours, those preceding dawn, that plants grow best, that they most increase in size. May this not be one of Nature's gentle showings to man of the times when he grows best, of the darkness of failure that is evolving into the sunlight of success. Let us fear only the failure of not living the right as we see it, leaving the results to the guardianship of the Infinite.

If we think of any supreme moment of our lives, any great success, anyone who is dear to us, and then consider how we reached that moment, that success, that friend, we will be surprised and strengthened by the revelation. As we trace each one back, step by step, through the genealogy of circumstances, we will see how logical has been the course of our joy and success from sorrow and failure, and that what gives us most happiness today is inextricably connected with what once caused us sorrow. Many of the rivers of our greatest prosperity and growth have had their source and their trickling increase into volume among the dark, gloomy recesses of our failure.

There is no honest and true work, carried along with constant and sincere purpose that ever really fails. If it sometimes seem to be wasted effort, it will prove to us a new lesson of "how" to walk; the secret of our failures will prove to us the inspiration of possible successes. Man living with the highest aims, ever as best he can, in continuous harmony with them, is a success, no matter what statistics of failure a near-sighted and half-blind world of critics and commentators may lay at his door.

High ideals, noble efforts will make seeming failures but trifles, they need not dishearten us; they should prove sources of new strength. The rocky way may prove safer than the slippery path of smoothness. Birds cannot fly best with the wind but against it; ships do not progress in calm, when the sails flap idly against the unstrained masts.

The alchemy of Nature, superior to that of the Paracelsians, constantly transmutes the baser metals of failure into the later pure gold of higher success, if the mind of the worker be kept true, constant, and untiring in the service, and he have that sublime courage that defies fate to its worst while he does his best.

XV

Doing Our Best *at* All Times

LIFE is a wondrously complex problem for the individual, until, some day, in a moment of illumination, he awakens to the great realization that he can make it simple,—never quite simple, but always simpler. There are a thousand mysteries of right and wrong that have baffled the wise men of the ages. There are depths in the great fundamental question of the human race that no plummet of philosophy has ever sounded. There are wild cries of honest hunger for truth that seek to pierce the silence beyond the grave, but to them ever echo back,—only a repetition of their unanswered cries.

To us all, comes, at times, the great note of questioning despair that darkens our horizon and paralyzes our effort:

"If there really be a God, if eternal justice really rule the world," we say, "why should life be as it is? Why do some men starve while others feast; why does virtue often languish in the shadow while vice triumphs in the sunshine; why does failure so often dog the footsteps of honest effort, while the success that comes from trickery and dishonor is greeted with the world's applause? How is it that the loving father of one family is taken by death, while the worthless incumbrance of another is spared? Why is there so much unnecessary pain, sorrowing and suffering in the world—why, indeed, should there be any?"

Neither philosophy nor religion can give any final satisfactory answer that is capable of logical demonstration, of absolute proof. There is ever, even after the best explanations, a residuum of the unexplained. We must then fall back in the eternal arms of faith, and be wise enough to say, "I will not be disconcerted by these problems of life, I will not permit them to plunge me into doubt, and to cloud my life with vagueness and uncertainty. Man arrogates much to himself when he demands from the infinite the full solution of all His mysteries. I will found my life on the impregnable rock of a simple fundamental truth: 'This glorious creation with its millions of wondrous phenomena pulsing ever in harmony with eternal law must have a Creator, that Creator must be omniscient and omnipotent. But that Creator Himself cannot, in justice, demand of any creature more than the best that that individual can give.' I will do each day, in every moment, the best I can by the light I have; I will ever seek more light, more perfect illumination of truth, and ever live as best I can in harmony with the truth as I see it. If failure come I will meet it bravely; if my pathway then lie in the shadow of trial, sorrow and suffering, I shall have the restful peace and the calm strength of one who has done his best, who can look back upon the past with no pang of regret, and who has heroic courage in facing the results, whatever they be, knowing that he could not make them different."

Upon this life-plan, this foundation, man may erect any superstructure of religion or philosophy that he conscientiously can erect; he should add to his equipment for living every shred of strength and inspiration, moral, mental, or spiritual that is in his power to secure.

This simple working faith is opposed to no creed, is a substitute for none; it is but a primary belief, a citadel, a refuge where the individual can retire for strength when the battle of life grows hard.

A mere theory of life, that remains but a theory, is about as useful to a man as a gilt-edged menu is to a starving sailor on a raft in mid-ocean. It is irritating but not stimulating. No rule for higher living will help a man in the slightest, until he reach out and appropriate it for himself, until he make it practical in his daily life, until that seed of theory in his mind blossom into a thousand flowers of thought and word and act

If a man honestly seek to live his best at all times, that determination is visible in every moment of his living, and no trifle in his life can be too insignificant to reflect his principle of living. The sun illuminates and beautifies a fallen leaf by the roadside as impartially as a towering mountain peak in the Alps. Every drop of water in the ocean is an epitome of the chemistry of the whole ocean; every drop is subject to precisely the same laws as dominate the united infinity of billions of drops that make that miracle of Nature, men call the Sea. No matter how humble the calling of the individual, how uninteresting and dull the round of his duties, he should do his best. He should dignify what he is doing by the mind he puts into it, he should vitalize what little he has of power or energy or ability or opportunity, in order to prepare himself to be equal to higher privileges when they come. This will never lead man to that weak content that is satisfied with whatever falls to his lot. It will rather fill his mind with that divine discontent that cheerfully accepts the best—merely as a temporary substitute for something better.

The man who is seeking ever to do his best is the man who is keen, active, wide-awake, and aggressive. He is ever watchful of himself in trifles; his standard is not "What will the world say?" but "Is it worthy of me?"

Edwin Booth, one of the greatest actors on the American stage, would never permit himself to assume an ungraceful attitude, even in his hours of privacy. In this simple thing, he ever lived his best. On the stage every move was one of unconscious grace. Those of his company who were conscious of their motions were the awkward ones, who were seeking in public to undo or to conceal the carelessness of the gestures and motions of their private life. The man who is slipshod and thoughtless in his daily speech, whose vocabulary is a collection of anæmic commonplaces, whose repetitions of phrases and extravagance of interjections act but as feeble disguises to his lack of ideas, will never be brilliant on an occasion when he longs to outshine the stars. Living at one's best is constant preparation for instant use. It can never make one over-precise, self-conscious, affected, or priggish. Education, in its highest sense, is *conscious* training of mind or body to act *unconsciously*. It is conscious formation of mental habits, not mere acquisition of information.

One of the many ways in which the individual unwisely eclipses himself, is in his worship of the fetich of luck. He feels that all others are lucky, and that whatever he attempts, fails. He does not realize the untiring energy, the unremitting concentration, the heroic courage, the sublime patience that is the secret of some men's success. Their "luck" was that they had prepared themselves to be equal to their opportunity when it came and were awake to recognize it and receive it. His own opportunity came and departed unnoted, it could not waken him from his dreams of some untold wealth that would fall into his lap. So he grows discouraged and envies those whom he should emulate, and he bandages his arms and chloroforms his energies, and performs his duties in a perfunctory way, or he passes through life, just ever "sampling" lines of activity.

The honest, faithful struggler should always realize that failure is but an episode in a true man's life—never the whole story. It is never easy to meet, and no philosophy can make it so, but the steadfast courage to master conditions, instead of complaining of them, will help him on his way; it will ever enable him to get the best out of what he has. He never knows the long series of vanquished failures that give solidity to someone else's success; he does not realize the price that some rich man, the innocent football of political malcontents and demagogues, has heroically paid for wealth and position.

The man who has a pessimist's doubt of all things; who demands a certified guarantee of his future; who ever fears his work will not be recognized or appreciated; or that after all, it is really not worth while, will never live his best. He is dulling his capacity for real progress by his hypnotic course of excuses for inactivity, instead of a strong tonic of reasons for action.

One of the most weakening elements in the individual make-up is the surrender to the oncoming of years. Man's self-confidence dims and dies in the fear of age. "This new thought," he says of some suggestion tending to higher development, "is good; it is what we need. I am glad to have it for my children; I would have been happy to have had some such help when I was at school, but it is too late for me. I am a man advanced in years."

This is but blind closing of life to wondrous possibilities. The knell of lost opportunity is never tolled in this life. It is never too late to recognize truth and to live by it. It requires only greater effort, closer attention, deeper consecration; but the impossible does not exist for the man who is self-confident and is willing to pay the price in time and struggle for his success or development. Later in life, the assessments are heavier in progress, as in life insurance, but that matters not to that mighty self-confidence that *will* not grow old while knowledge can keep it young.

Socrates, when his hair whitened with the snow of age, learned to play on instruments of music. Cato, at fourscore, began his study of Greek, and the same age saw Plutarch beginning, with the enthusiasm of a boy, his first lessons in Latin. The Character of Man, Theophrastus' greatest work, was begun on his ninetieth birthday. Chaucer's Canterbury Tales was the work of the poet's declining years. Ronsard, the father of French poetry, whose sonnets even translation cannot destroy, did not develop his poetic faculty until nearly fifty. Benjamin Franklin at this age had just taken his really first steps of importance in philosophic pursuits. Arnauld, the theologian and sage, translated Josephus in his eightieth year. Winckelmann, one of the most famous writers on classic antiquities, was the son of a shoemaker, and lived in obscurity and ignorance until the prime of life. Hobbes, the English philosopher, published his version of the Odyssey in his eighty-seventh year, and his Iliad one year later. Chevreul, the great French scientist, whose untiring labors in the realm of color have so enriched the world, was busy, keen and active when Death called him, at the age of 103.

These men did not fear age; these few names from the great muster-roll of the famous ones who defied the years, should be voices of hope and heartening to every individual whose courage and confidence is weak. The path of truth, higher living, truer development in every phase of life, is never shut from the individual—until he closes it himself. Let man feel this, believe it and make this faith a real and living factor in his life and there are no limits to his progress. He has but to live his best at all times, and rest calm and untroubled no matter what results come to his efforts. The constant looking backward to what might have been, instead of forward to what may be, is a great weakener of self-confidence. This worry for the old past, this wasted energy, for that which no power in the world can restore, ever lessens the individual's faith in himself, weakens his efforts to develop himself for the future to the perfection of his possibilities.

Nature in her beautiful love and tenderness, says to man, weakened and worn and weary with the struggle, "Do in the best way you can the trifle that is under your hand at this moment; do it in the best spirit of preparation for the future your thought suggests; bring all the light of knowledge from all the past to aid you. Do this and you have done your best. The past is forever closed to you. It is closed forever to you.

No worry, no struggle, no suffering, no agony of despair can alter it. It is as much beyond your power as if it were a million years of eternity behind you. Turn all that past, with its sad hours, weakness and sin, its wasted opportunities as light, in confidence and hope, upon the future. Turn it all in fuller truth and light so as to make each trifle of this present a new past it will be joy to look back to; each trifle a grander, nobler, and more perfect preparation for the future. The present and the future you can make from it, is yours; the past has gone back, with all its messages, all its history, all its records to the God who loaned you the golden moments to use in obedience to His law.

XVI

The Royal Road *to* Happiness

DURING my whole life I have not had twenty-four hours of happiness." So said Prince Bismarck, one of the greatest statesmen of the nineteenth century. Eighty-three years of wealth, fame, honors, power, influence, prosperity and triumph,—years when he held an empire in his fingers,—but not one day of happiness!

Happiness is the greatest paradox in Nature. It can grow in any soil, live under any conditions. It defies environment. It comes from within; it is the revelation of the depths of the inner life as light and heat proclaim the sun from which they radiate. Happiness consists not of having, but of being; not of possessing, but of enjoying. It is the warm glow of a heart at peace with itself. A martyr at the stake may have happiness that a king on his throne might envy. Man is the creator of his own happiness; it is the aroma of a life lived in harmony with high ideals. For what a man *has*, he may be dependent on others; what he *is*, rests with him alone. What he *ob*tains in life is but acquisition; what he *at*tains, is growth. Happiness is the soul's joy in the possession of the intangible. Absolute, perfect, continuous happiness in life, is impossible for the human. It would mean the consummation of attainments, the individual consciousness of a perfectly fulfilled destiny. Happiness is paradoxic because it may co-exist with trial, sorrow and poverty. It is the gladness of the heart rising superior to all conditions.

Happiness has a number of under-studies,—gratification, satisfaction, content and pleasure,—clever imitators that simulate its appearance rather than emulate its method. Gratification is a harmony between our desires and our possessions. It is ever incomplete, it is the thankful acceptance of part. It is a mental pleasure in the quality of what one receives, an unsatisfiedness as to the quantity. It may be an element in happiness, but, in itself,—it is not happiness.

Satisfaction is perfect identity of our desires and our possessions. It exists only so long as this perfect union and unity can be preserved. But every realized ideal gives birth to new ideals, every step in advance reveals large domains of the unattained; every feeding stimulates new appetites—then the desires and possessions are no longer identical, no longer equal; new cravings call forth new activities, the equipoise is destroyed, and dissatisfaction reënters. Man might possess everything tangible in the world and yet not be happy, for happiness is the satisfying of the soul, not of the mind or the body. Dissatisfaction, in its highest sense, is the keynote of all advance, the evidence of new aspirations, the guarantee of the progressive revelation of new possibilities.

Content is a greatly overrated virtue. It is a kind of diluted despair; it is the feeling with which we continue to accept substitutes, without striving for the realities. Content makes the trained individual swallow vinegar and try to smack his lips as if it were wine. Content enables one to warm his hands at the fire of a past joy that exists only in memory. Content is a mental and moral chloroform that deadens the activities of the individual to rise to higher planes of life and growth. Man should never be contented with anything less than the best efforts of his nature can possibly secure for him. Content makes the world more comfortable for the individual, but it is the death-knell of progress. Man should be content with each step of progress merely as a station, discontented with it as a destination; contented with it as a step; discontented with it as a finality. There are times when a man should be content with what he *has*, but never with what he *is*.

But content is not happiness; neither is pleasure. Pleasure is temporary, happiness is continuous; pleasure is a note, happiness is a symphony; pleasure may exist when conscience utters protests; happiness, never. Pleasure may have its dregs and its lees; but none can be found in the cup of happiness.

Man is the only animal that can be really happy. To the rest of the creation belong only weak imitations of the understudies. Happiness represents a peaceful attunement of a life with a standard of living. It can never be made by the individual, by himself, for himself. It is one of the incidental by-products of an unselfish life. No man can make his own happiness the one object of his life and attain it, any more than he can jump on the far end of his shadow. If you would hit the bull's-eye of happiness on the target of life, aim above it. Place other things higher than your own happiness and it will surely come to you. You can buy pleasure, you can acquire content, you can become satisfied,—but Nature never put real happiness on the bargain-counter. It is the undetachable accompaniment of true living. It is calm and peaceful; it never lives in an atmosphere of worry or of hopeless struggle.

The basis of happiness is the love of something outside self. Search every instance of happiness in the world, and you will find, when all the incidental features are eliminated, there is always the constant, unchangeable element of love,—love of parent for child; love of man and woman for each other; love of humanity in some form, or a great life work into which the individual throws all his energies.

Happiness is the voice of optimism, of faith, of simple, steadfast love. No cynic or pessimist can be really happy. A cynic is a man who is morally near-sighted,—and brags about it. He sees the evil in his own heart, and thinks he sees the world. He lets a mote in his eye eclipse the sun. An incurable cynic is an individual who should long for death,—for life cannot bring him happiness, death might. The keynote of Bismarck's lack of happiness was his profound distrust of human nature.

There is a royal road to happiness; it lies in Consecration, Concentration, Conquest and Conscience.

Consecration is dedicating the individual life to the service of others, to some noble mission, to realizing some unselfish ideal. Life is not something to be lived *through;* it is something to be lived *up* to. It is a privilege, not a penal servitude of so many decades on earth. Consecration places the object of life above the mere acquisition of money, as a finality. The man who is unselfish, kind, loving, tender, helpful, ready to lighten the burden of those around him, to hearten the struggling ones, to forget himself sometimes in remembering others, is on the right road to happiness. Consecration is ever active, bold and aggressive, fearing naught but possible disloyalty to high ideals.

Concentration makes the individual life simpler and deeper. It cuts away the shams and pretences of modern living and limits life to its truest essentials. Worry, fear, useless regret—all the great wastes that sap mental, moral or physical energy—must be sacrificed, or the individual needlessly destroys half the possibilities of living. A great purpose in life, something that unifies the strands and threads of each day's thinking, something that takes the sting from the petty trials, sorrows, sufferings and blunders of life, is a great aid to Concentration. Soldiers in battle may forget their wounds, or even be unconscious of them, in the inspiration of battling for what they believe is right. Concentration dignifies an humble life; it makes a great life,—sublime. In morals it is a short-cut to simplicity. It leads to right for right's sake, without thought of policy or of reward. It brings calm and rest to the individual,—a serenity that is but the sunlight of happiness.

Conquest is the overcoming of an evil habit, the rising superior to opposition and attack, the spiritual exaltation that comes from resisting the invasion of the grovelling material side of life. Sometimes when you are worn and weak with the struggle; when it seems that justice is a dream, that honesty and loyalty and truth count for nothing, that the devil is the only good paymaster; when hope grows dim and flickers, then is the time when you must tower in the great sublime faith that Right must prevail, then must you throttle these imps of doubt and despair, you must master yourself to master the world around you. This is Conquest; this is what counts. Even a log can float with the current, it takes a man to fight sturdily against an opposing tide that would sweep his craft out of its course. When the jealousies, the petty intrigues and the meannesses and the misunderstandings in life assail you, rise above them. Be like a lighthouse that illumines and beautifies the snarling, swashing waves of the storm that threaten it, that seek to undermine it and seek to wash over it. This is Conquest. When the chance to win fame, wealth, success or the attainment of your heart's desire, by sacrifice of honor or principle, comes to you and it does not affect you long enough even to seem a temptation, you have been the victor. That too is Conquest. And Conquest is part of the royal road to Happiness.

Conscience, as the mentor, the guide and compass of every act, leads ever to Happiness. When the individual can stay alone with his conscience and get its approval, without using force or specious logic, then he begins to know what real Happiness is. But the individual must be careful that he is not appealing to a conscience perverted or deadened by the wrongdoing and consequent deafness of its owner. The man who is honestly seeking to live his life in Consecration, Concentration and Conquest, living from day to day as best he can, by the light he has, may rely implicitly on his Conscience. He can shut his ears to "what the world says" and find in the approval of his own conscience the highest earthly tribune—the voice of the Infinite communing with the Individual.

Unhappiness is the hunger to get; Happiness is the hunger to give. True happiness must ever have the tinge of sorrow outlived, the sense of pain softened by the mellowing years, the chastening of loss that in the wondrous mystery of time transmutes our suffering into love and sympathy with others.

If the individual should set out for a single day to give Happiness, to make life happier, brighter and sweeter, not for himself, but for others, he would find a wondrous revelation of what Happiness really is. The greatest of the world's heroes could not by any series of acts of heroism do as much real good as any individual living his whole life in seeking, from day to day, to make others happy.

Each day there should be fresh resolution, new strength, and renewed enthusiasm. "Just for To-day" might be the daily motto of thousands of societies through the country, composed of members bound together to make the world better through constant simple acts of kindness, constant deeds of sweetness and love. And Happiness would come to them, in its highest and best form, not because they would seek to *absorb* it, but—because they seek to *radiate* it.